Unorthodox

Unorthodox

Poems of Winter, Christmas and Hanukkah

KYLE JANKOWSKI

FOREWORD & EDITED BY
CLIFFORD MAYES

First English Edition: December 2024

Cover Art: *Annunciation*, mosaic tile mural at National Shrine of Our Lady of the Snows, Belleville, Illinois. http://snows.org. Photo by Kyle Jankowski (© 2022).

Bible translations used: New Jerusalem Bible (NJB), New Jerusalem Version (NJV), New International Version (NIV), Douay-Rheims (DRB).

Siubhail Publishing, LLC, USA
www.siubhailpublishingllc.com

via Amazon Kindle Direct Publishing

CHARITABLE DONATIONS DISCLOSURE

A percentage of profits from the sale of this book will be donated to support impoverished children's education.

MORE BOOKS BY
KYLE JANKOWSKI

"The Poet as Archetypal Teacher in Unteachable Times"
in
New Visions and new Voices: Extending the Principles of Archetypal Psychology to Include a Variety of Venues, Issues, and Projects (Vol. 2)
-(Eds.) Clifford Mayes & Jacqueline Ann Rinaldi
In print Spring 2023, Roman and Littlefield Publishers

Dispatches from the Dnipro:
Poems on the War in Ukraine
(Ed.) Clifford Mayes
In print 2023, Siubhail Publishing, LLC
Available on amazon.com

The Mermaid and Her Sword:
New Polish Proverbs for Perilous Times
-(Ed. & Commentary) Clifford Mayes
In print 2025, Siubhail Publishing, LLC
Available on amazon.com

Kyle's poetry has regularly appeared in *An Darag*, a quarterly zine of American Scottish Clan Hamilton Society, of which he is a member.

To contact the author directly, or for more information on upcoming projects, release dates, requests for poetry readings, lectures, teach-ins, workshops or presentations, please visit www.siubhailpublishingllc.com.

PROFESSIONAL LEGAL DISCLAIMER

The websites, emails, review/comment/posting boards or other contact information are *not* a contact for professional psychotherapy services. Reading this book does not constitute a therapeutic relationship or as professional therapy advice, neither does "fan" correspondence, or academic coordination. All opinions in this collection are my own and do not reflect the opinions or positions of any organization or group with which I am affiliated, or other individuals named in this book. Though great attention to detail, research, accuracy and sensitivity have been used while creating this poetry and it's scholarly content, any mistakes or errors are my own.

To the Untier of Knots

Acknowledgements

Grandmother Jankowski, for unapologetically modeling the spirit of Christmas love. My wife, Vanessa, who blends complex and at times conflicting, heritage into simple traditions and joys. Fr. Mike, for his encouragement to bring newer, younger, Midwestern and blue-collar voices back into modern Catholic/ Christian literature and mysticism—voices grounded in and informed by history, and inspired by the best of our collective traditions. Special thanks to my editor, Clifford Mayes, and also my late mentors, for helping me build an inner Jerusalem, where all traditions can coexist, and thrive. Also thanks to fellow saxophonists—Derek Hinderliter, twenty-year Air Force Band veteran, and psychotherapist, for the many energizing and engaging chats about music as medicine—and Dr. Adrianne Honnold, Professor of Musicology and veteran of the Air Force Band, for her expertise in American jazz, popular music culture and history. Finally, but not least, my Jewish, Muslim, Hindu and Buddhist clients and friends, who have shared their surprising personal appreciations of Classical Christian traditions, teachings, music, symbolism, imagery and art.

Content

Foreword

The Poem as Hospitality in the Recent Work of Kyle Jankowski

Clifford Mayes
Professor (Emeritus)
Educational Psychology
Brigham Young University

"All guests who present themselves are to be welcomed as Christ."

St. Benedict, *Rules of the Benedictine Order*

As both a psychotherapist with a graduate degree as a clinician from the University of Chicago's celebrated School of Social Work and as a highly perceptive student of Carl Jung's archetypal psychology with another graduate degree from the premier program in Jungian psychology in the United States, Pacifica Graduate Institute, it should come as no surprise that one of the features of Jankowski's poetry is his experiences and perspectives as a Jungian-oriented therapist at the clinic he runs with his wife, Dr. Vanessa Jankowski, near Chicago. He explores them in their daunting variety, grinding pain, and poignancy intermixed and occasional absurdity, in this volume of his most recent work.

This is not to say, however, that his poetry is reducible to some kind of poetic exposition of a school of psychology or even of "a day in the life of a Jungian therapist." As I have noted elsewhere (Mayes 2023), Jankowski's poetry covers so much ground and is so unique that it would give the reader of Jankowski a skewed idea of his total project to suggest that just this one aspect of it, however prominent, is the whole story. Having said that, however, I must, given the space limitations of this brief foreword, confine myself to an aspect of his work, and this aspect seems to me a good entree into his multifaceted opus.

I have noted elsewhere that Jankowski is a poet *sui generis*-one of a kind. But that is not to say that there are no influences or precedents in Jankowski's work. Of course, there are. There must be. Poetry, like most important things, is always a question of context. Thus, like most serious poets, Jankowski draws from his environment to provide his work with what Shakespeare called "a local habitation and a name" (A Midsummer Night's Dream, Act V, Scene 1). But, like those poets, he also will not allow himself to be limited by context. Otherwise, he or she winds up being, as T.S. Eliot called William Carlos Williams (in a classic instance of damning by faint praise) "an interesting local poet"--but nothing more. The poet transcends his or her immediate environment to attain a higher perspective.

This is crucial. It attends to the famous dictum, generally attributed to Einstein, that a seemingly insoluble problem can never be figured out on the plane of thinking at which it was generated. And a poem, if it is a good poem, must always be a problem for the reader to resolve that cannot be negotiated in any other way than by the unique medium of the poem–with its pregnant ambiguities, polyvalent symbols, and multiple but simultaneous perspectives that grant the poet and the reader access into realms of meaning that ordinary discursive language is simply not up to providing. The poet and reader thereby grow as complex human beings in the process.

Thus, a poem, or any existential problem of complexity and merit, which inevitably contains a tension to be worked with and worked through, must, itself, be a relocation of the problem to a higher plane. Picture a triangle, with two opposing views on some matter of great importance being the two poles of the base. The apex of the triangle is the place where the dialectical tension gets resolved in an ethically more complete vision that neither pole of the base was ever designed to achieve.

This transformation of conflict at a lower plane into conciliation at a higher plane is a dynamic that Jung called "the trans-cendent function," and it is at the very heart of Jungian theory and therapy (Miller 2004), which is all about the reconciliation of opposites within the individual. Synching all these opposites within oneself into a coherent whole, where the sum is qualitatively greater than the ontological sum of the parts, is what Jung called "individuation." It is the goal of Jungian theory and therapy (Miller 2004).

What I am driving at here is that in Unorthodox, we see this process of the transcendent function in the service of individuation in full swing. It is a process that generally starts around midlife (Mr. Jankowski just turned forty)—if, that is, individuation is to start at all. For although it is talked about a great deal in Jungian academic circles, individuation is actually a rare thing according to Jung (1960), Individuation requires bringing opposites within oneself together into a coherent and vital whole. It is not just a psychological task but a spiritual one that fructifies in wisdom and empathy, which is finally a simple and satisfying way of picturing individuation. It is attainable only through "prayer, observance, discipline, thought, and action." (Eliot 1970, *Four Quartets*, "Little Gidding"). It is a lifelong task. It is, in fact, a calling–one which Jankowski has clearly responded to with enormous authenticity in *Unorthodox*.

The themes of the poems in *Unorthodox* evidence many of the same dialectical tensions that one sees in his earlier work. Jankowski is a multifaceted man, and many contrarieties power his work. But it has ever been thus if a poem is to be interesting and its resolution *by* the individual reader to be "educative" *for* the individual reader (Eagleton, 2011), who will appropriate it in his or her own way (Mayes and Savage, in press). Hence, we see many of the same tensions that informed his earlier poetry shaping this volume. For, Mr. Jankowski's work comprises a panoply of issues in addition to those that present themselves to him on a daily basis in his consulting room. These include (but are not limited to) the slow and awful crumbling of Western culture in the wake of the wrecking ball of postmodernism in academia, and the resulting vacuums in young adults' souls. These multiple generations, who through post-modernism, feel and believe they have absolutely nothing to believe in (some more tragically, believe there is also no reason to live). His work is furthered by the defoliating effects on the ancient lands and the deracinating effects on the ancient cultures through the "McDonaldization" of the world by international corporate capitalism. Mr. Jankowski is keenly aware of the problems, and possibilities, of the 2000-year-old Roman Catholicism—especially in his devotion to the *Theotokos,* the Mother of God, who is his frequent companion and occasional muse, and is enormously important in his psychic and spiritual economy. All of this, and more, makes of Jankowski an unlikely poet in our jaded times and, therefore, just the kind of voice we need to hear to get us reoriented and restored. But it is to Mr. Jankowski the therapist that I am primarily turning here.

Now, one of those foundational tensions in Jankowski's work is between his naturally conservative nature and a liberal outlook and sympathy cultivated by means of his years of graduate work at the University of Chicago and Pacifica—both bastions of Progressive outlooks. In *Unorthodox*, Jankowski presents us with an empathetic blend of both worldviews—a transcendent function, achieved and embodied in and as the poetry itself. The poem, in other words, now *is* the transcendent function that harmonizes the Progressive world-view with the Conservative one. In his earlier poetry, one feels the weighty passion of the conflict sometimes eating away at him. One

---

16

agonizes with him as he searches for a solution to the fine mess we have gotten ourselves into as a culture.

In *Unorthodox,* the reader is invited to settle into a realistic, more relaxed, and generative vision that does not strive for a solution so much as it invites us to live with the contrarieties, in a way that vexes us less and moves us more in the direction of a new, shared vision, whatever that may turn out to be and however we may be compelled to evolve in its realization.

But Jankowski is the last thing from a glib idealist. A son of the Rust Belt's conservative Polish Blue-Collar class, he sees and (more to the point) *feels* the dread personally, and even more dire, feels, and takes us the readers into, the world-historical effects that the demise of our traditions, and those of our neighbors and country men and women, have on us. We are all in the same boat together—a historically impoverished and spiritually rudderless group of bewildered sailors adrift and akimbo on the wanton waves of capricious, tormented times. Writes Jankowski in "Christmas Eve, 2023":

> Preparing to host a tableful and home full of guests—
> Catholics,
> Protestants,
> Gnostics,
> Pagans,
> the spiritually unaffiliated,
> post-Christians—
> I see the news break about the Holy Land.
> Christmas, the gathering of fellowship in peace,
> Canceled.
> A curious act of "solidarity"....
> As it is said about the true meaning of poem, look to
> the text, not what the poet says about it. I continue
> mixing beet salad, hands looking bloodied, and begin
> quietly singing.
>
> O *come all ye faithful, to Bethlehem...*
> (to the empty churches)
> *Oh come oh come Emmanuel, and ransom captive Israel* ,
> (among the gullible and ahistorical does propaganda easily
>   travel)
> *That mourns in lonely exile here.*
> (where all the tired hatred tropes appear.)
> *To us the path of knowledge show...*
> (which does not from the river to the sea flow)
> *From the depths of hell your people save*

(from those who turn the Religion of Peace into a quick path
       to the grave)
Oh come o bright and speak to us as *Sayyida Siddiquah*
Dispel the shadows of the night
(each nation's apathy and ignorance is our collective plight)
Bid our sad divisions cease.

Yet, in all this, he neither preaches nor temporizes—a flaw in some of his earlier poetry. Staying true to his principles, he now sees things not so much in dichotomies but in terms of a feast to which all are invited. Indeed, both giving and attending dinners is a *leitmotif* in *Unorthodox*. I am reminded of when Jesus speaks of a wedding banquet, a somehow final and culminating event sponsored by a great king upon his return from a distant land. Here is the apocalyptic Jankowski, who carries on what Dylan Thomas called the poet's "craft or sullen art" (2000) under the funeral pull of what Kermode (1967) called the "sense of an ending." But in our parables the people whom the king had previously invited now refuse, for one spurious reason or other, to come to this climactic event at the end of history. This leaves those who had previously been ignored, marginalized, even disdained as the new guests in the new banquet, a paradoxical feast on the difficult contradictions that living in our knotted-up and contested times entails. Here, Jankowski sagaciously offers not so much "solutions" as the opportunity to rest in the contradictions, and simply learn to live with each other. He entreats all the persons involved in contested communications to listen to each other's ideas with as much respect as they can still genuinely muster; respond to all the ideas.

Then—in perhaps the most powerful line in this volume, which has no shortage of memorable lines, Jankowski declares that "We satirize the traditions because we have forgotten how to be together" ("A Pagan, a Christian and a Post-Christian Modern Walk into a Recording Studio with Kabir and C.S. Lewis").

Here, at last, in the final poem in the volume, is the key. We must each, as much as is possible, rehabilitate our old traditions, the fountainhead of any sagacity and love we can hope to acquire in this life, and through profound and mutually respectful dialogue, each share what we have to offer in order to forge new myths to carry us forward in what Dewey called "a common faith" that must underlie a democracy. Otherwise, that culture will promiscuously fall into a decaying orbit, devolve into vapid cynicism, self-destructive and egregious practices, and get fatally off track and begin to wander in a miasma of alienation so profound that we have lost the ability to see our way forward because we have lost the ability to see each other.

Writes Jankowski with a tenderness that evidences his increasing degrees of individuation, which, looked at from one angle, is nothing more but also nothing less than a waxing capacity for compassion:

Those over-sung carols, they will not bring you joy.
But there are meta-verses whose
Meaning presently escapes you.
Slow your holiday (and daily) rush.
They are in plain sight.
You must listen more deeply
for long-unsung carols and chants,
Some forgotten,
Some your grandparents barely recalled when they were young.
Others perhaps sung in a tongue your grandparents-
        grandparents forgot
Before they left primary school.
That sardonic and cynical humor will not soothe your sad
        condition.
We satirize the traditions because we have forgotten how to be
        together.
But mockery is a poor lock pick
To break the tension
Restraining your hearts' tongue.
Dear ones, stop
Feigning tolerance, which is just a pantomime of love.
Throughout the year, cease
Dedicating your studies to learning what Kabir calls "terrific
        talking."
Both of these shut iron gates to the heart–
A heart empty of song.

At this point, the *axis mundi* of the volume, Jankowski the psychotherapist merges with Jankowski the conservative progressive and progressive conservative, makes common cause with Jankowski the scholar wedded to Jankowski the poet, identifies with Jankowski the social critic hand in hand with Jankowski the monastic Catholic, and echoes the same liberating cry that Jankowski the Slavic patriot and Jankowski the new advocate of a common faith sing in a harmony of many parts. So many of his many voices in his previous work achieve a contrapuntal climax in this slender, elegant, and authoritative volume.

This beautiful instance of individuation, this concourse of paths within the soul of the poet that he offers up for the edification of his reader's own psycho-spiritual growth, this nearly eighty-page long poetic witness to the restoration of the older traditions concurrently with the creation of new mythologems (which, not incidentally, was also Jung's life-project)—this, and more, is all available within the covers of this seasonal volume that is, finally, a book for all seasons, by (in my estimation) one of our most promising new poets–Kyle Jankowski. This new hospitality that each of his poems offers each of his readers–kindles, paradoxically and precisely, when we all also feel in the very same instant, the first soot from the volcano of apocalyptic times falling on our furrowed brows. *Kyrie eleison.* We need the poetry of Kyle Jankowski.

References

Eagleton, T. (2011). *Literary Theory: An Introduction.* Wiley-Blackwell.

Eliot, T.S. (1970). *The Complete Poems and Plays of T.S. Eliot.* Harcourt and Brace.

Jung, C.G. (1960). *The Undiscovered Self.* Free Press

Kermode, F. (1967). *The Sense of an Ending: Studies in the Theory of Fiction.* Oxford University Press.

Mayes, Clifford; Rinaldi, Jacqueline Ann (2023). "The Poet as Archetypal Teacher in Unteachable Times". *New Visions and New Voices: Extending the Principles of Archetypal Psychology to Include a Variety of Venues, Issues, and Projects (Vol. 2).* Roman & Littlefield Publishers.

Mayes, Clifford; Savage, Claire (in press). *Jung's Transcendent Function: The Shadow and Symbol in Teaching and Learning.*

Miller, J. (2004). *The transcendent function: Jung's model of psychological growth through dialogue with the unconscious.* State University of New York Press.

Thomas, D. (2000). "In My Craft or Sullen Art" in *The Collected Poems of Dylan Thomas.* Yale University Press.

Introduction

Hymns to Cultural Complexes and Personal Shadow Work: Renewing and Respecting Winter Holiday Traditions Through Music

Kyle Jankowski

"There are no questions more urgent than the naïve ones."

-Wislawa Szymborska, "Turn of the 20th Century"

I was not raised with poetry or poets being discussed at the dinner table, BBQs, family parties or among friends. Committing great time, energy and resources in the middle third and second-half half of my life to writing poetry books is an unusual choice. Poetry expresses the inner life or what is referred to in theology and Depth Psychology (Jungian, Freudian and Archetypal) as the soul. Music is one of poetry's many well-tuned forms. The collective state of Christmas and other Winter Holiday's music echoes the state of a society's collective psychological state. This poetry is my response—as a member of my generation, as a therapist, a social worker, and an American—to these issues.

Also publishing print books, when it appears an exponential number of people, especially in young America, no longer read, or have attention span to learn anything aside from their preferred "content". Yet across the current generations, there is also a strong desire to slowdown and reclaim private space and time from our manic-tech-info-hyper-connection lifestyles. Routines that have been pressed upon us by self-appointed visionaries and techno-prophets, and plug-in-or-you-can't-play economics. This Winter Holiday's poetry collection is first an opportunity, then a tool, for slowing and reclaiming your wintertime life.

Work on this book began nearly a decade ago, about the time I began serious attempts again to write poetry. Personal grief work (several of my mentors had recently died) initiated this new composition. Shortly it transformed into a more dedicated approach to clinical psycho-therapy *through* poetry. Designing half-a-dozen professional and personal growth workshops followed, arranged around poetry, to engage groups of participants in what is now popularly termed "Shadow Work". Shadow Work is based on the famous Swiss Psychologist Carl Jung's (C.G. Jung) concept of the Transcendent Function, where two seemingly opposite points create a demand to transform our perspective, to transcend the conflict, and find a meeting place, the middle third. By doing so, our perspective and understanding is widened and bridges the gaps.

This is working between the lines, finding the enharmonic tones between discordant and dissonant tunings, dancing among paradoxes, seeking to resolve what Jung termed the "tension of opposites", the "ultimate phase" of shadow work.[1] But it was through music that I came to psychology, fascinated by people's stories, and from there to poetry. Then in my senior year of college, one of my clinical fieldwork professors began using poetry to teach us about the practices of social work, case management and psychotherapy.[2] I was fascinated but also unsure of poetry's place in a world constantly droning with music. So until about a decade ago, I selected music over poetry as my favorite therapeutic and educational tool.

Music in the Family

In abundance, my classmates, friends and I did hear, share and debate what literary elites have often smugly insisted is the "lower" poetry; music. Mixed genre tunes—"oldies", Classic Rock, Blues, Hip Hop, Top 40 Pop, Jazz, 90s Country—were playing in virtually every business, building, and establishment I frequented during my youth. Some eagerly explored, others dragged through. Record stores, pawn shops, the DMV, music lessons, swimming practice, Boy Scouts, school. Also my father's circuit—fast-food restaurants, Murray's (now O'Reilly's) Auto Parts, hardware stores, Meijer's grocery, school, the Post Office. And mother's favorites routines—Hallmark Shops, bookstores, nursery and garden centers, the Post Office, shopping malls, and her employer, the county hospital. I have practiced saxophone since age twelve, playing in every ensemble and group from primary school to college. Now I'm endeavoring to befriend the Great Highland Bagpipes. Through music I first learned to listen intently and patiently, allowing the tones to tell whichever story was written on staff paper, and transcribe the sonic lines into images parading through my inner world, memories, imagination, and taking me "through the looking glass".

My maternal grandfather, a combat veteran of WWII (China-Burma-India Theater), a computer engineer at General Motors, Scottish Pipe and Drum Band drummer, and concert percussionist, introduced me to the Mormon Tabernacle Choir, BBC Proms (via National Public Radio), Boston Symphony Orchestra Holiday Pops, the Canadian Brass, the Salvation Army Band, Russian State Symphony spiriting ballet dancers floating through Tchaikovsky's Nutcracker Suite, and Pavarotti bellowing Handel's Messiah and Schubert's Ave Maria, *in full 10,000 watt stereo.*

Growing up around Eastern and Northern Michigan there is a sizable influence, though at times more "background music", of Canadian, Celtic (Scots-Irish, Welsh) cultures. Many of my grade school teachers still taught American and European and British Commonwealth classics as part of curriculum interspersed with a classic liberal-arts education, in which Anglo/Celtic heritage music, poetry, and literature was included. Through them, and attending Catholic and Protestant services, I memorized to heart the verses of the old carols and hymns. It was through music , liturgical and contemporary, that I learned the Gospels and Jewish books of the Torah and Old Testament, but not from formal Bible study Catechism (Catholic Sunday School). After all, the Psalms were meant to be sung poetry, not dryly recited like Jeopardy factoids.

This was before such Western classics were put on "black lists", deemed threatening to the latest Avant Garde "progress" revolution. Polish culture and history were of course never included as part of formal education, and still aren't Many of us familiar with Polish history from the past five-hundred-years do not wonder why this is ongoing phenomenon is so. Our American education system also has always been Anglo-Franco-Prussian based and focused, and now has evolved to include Afro, Asian and Latino-centric education, but Slavic culture remains elusive.

Community is Always Improvised Harmony

In my section of the slower-changing, but still reliably innovative, American Midwest (Michigan and Illinois), Canadian and Anglo/British-Celtic culture was (and to some degree is) steadfastly infused into the primary education system, integrated with conservative and progressive American culture and principles. Most of my multi-ethnic teachers were veterans of the American Civil Rights Movements, WWII, Korea, Vietnam, and Gulf War. They were American Blacks, Choctaw, Germans, Polish, Scots-Irish, etc., and had not been indoctrinated or "properly educated" to mock, belittle, or wholesale ignore the *positive* aspects of Celtic/Anglo culture's (or any other cultures') contributions to America and the human accomplishment and heritage. Their opinions and principles *did not* echo of internalized "isms", but did regularly distribute intellectually honest and often harsh critiques all around. These Teachers taught and disciplined by "content of character", not color of skin (À LA Dr. Martin Luther King), and by principles and Truth, not popular propaganda. They endeavored and innovated instructional methods to help us to understand, appreciate, and account for, our own history, culture and principles, before idealizing (or shaming) the foreign and exotic.

Thus, my Teachers did give the now popularly-derided Euro/Western cultures a respected place on the "*community* concert stage", *side-by-side* with American Black, Creole, Native American, Latino/Hispanic, Jewish, Persian and Egyptian. Even if the later groups were given the leadership positions and honored guests' seats for the time being, the melody made its way around the whole group, and everyone got the opportunity to step forward and risk showing their best and worst skills at improvising the bridges. We are all just improvising before the Divine. God is a trickster Who loves to improvise Classical *and* Chicago/Delta Blues. Want to make the higher power laugh? Make a plan that doesn't include improvisation.

I don't include South Asian, pan-African, Australian/Oceanic, or other Arabic cultures in these particular recollections simply because, at the time of my youth (1980s-early 2000s), they had extremely small physical and cultural presence in my part of the Midwest (Flint, Michigan). Yet since those times, Detroit's "Little Warsaw" and Polish dominant Hamtramck have traded Kielbasa for Kebabs, part of the *inevitable* ever-changing, *transforming*, American Experiment. This poetry collection is my answer to cultural pluralism and embracing mutual appreciation among our neighbors during the Winter Holidays. I found particular difficulty locating corresponding Arabic (particularly Islamic) traditions in the Winter cycle. This is challenging due to the rotating dates of Islamic religious holidays and associated practices.

The Islamic calendar is lunar cycle based. Though most Muslims recognize Jesus of Nazareth by many titles of esteem, Ramadan is celebrated as the highest Muslim holiday. Ramadan sometimes falls during Fall/Winter, but not consistently. My Muslim patients and neighbors affirmed this dissonant custom as a frustrating barrier to cultural synchronization and a social integration barrier when living in non-Islamic law structured cultures. In curious contrast, Western and Orthodox Christmas, shamanic/animist Winter Solstice, Cherokee *Tsalagi*, Hanukkah, Kwanzaa, Diwali, Buddhism's Bodhi Day, Taoist Dōngzhì festival, Zoroastrian *Jashn-e Sadeh*, Jainism's *Pausha Dashmi* (Winter Solstice) and *Makar Sankranti*, Chinese New Year and other traditions all *annually* occur in late Autumn/ Winter, matching the familiar Advent/Christmas cycle's date range.

Most of these holidays are not featured in this collection because as a storyteller, I am currently not familiar enough to respectfully address them, but future collections may feature them. In the meantime, I enthusiastically encourage you readers who have kinship with these other traditions, religions and creeds to endeavor to compose your own poetry, prose, film, and song to honor your celebrations and holidays.

The Lean Months

Several generations of America did not write much new music for the Winter Holidays, including for Christmas, Hanukkah, pagan Winter Solstice, or secular observance of general national Holidays. Though many millions of dollars have been spent re-recording classics that were inked to staff paper centuries ago, or written in New Orleans, New York and Chicago apartments during what's referred to as golden years—1920s, 30s and 40s. In the mean-time, Black America continued to innovatively express their, and our, collective Winter experiences, dismal and joyful.

James Brown's disco/R&B inspired album, "Soulful Christmas", especially the track, *Santa Claus Go Straight to the Ghetto* (J. Brown, H. Ballard, A.J. Ellis) was, and still is, a serious artistic "community service", reminding listeners about Winter's historical harshness, even still in modern society with modern tech. Brown's performance acknowledges the poverty and material suffering poor communities keenly experience during the "lean months". It's "the most wonderful time of the year", when wage and contract hours get cut, temp retail jobs are available (or not) at the whim of upper middle-class and wealthy folk's spending habits and corporate sales projections, bonuses come up short, and somehow the promised profit-sharing never seems to fully materialize. There's also the seasonal physical depression piled on from Vitamin-D and sun deficiency, nutrition-deficit comfort eating, sugar spiking/crashing, or worse diabetes-making diets, general physical activity slowdown and social isolation.

In the rural Rust Belt, as well as the large urban ghettos, and even middle neighborhoods, we all feel—some agonizingly more than others—another annual year-end disappointment. Promised and much politically lauded business and financial investment and community redevelopment that never seems to happen. The self-congratulatory trickle-down economics that has had a nearly fifty-year innovation drought. The much-lauded social welfare programs that target what feels good to donors and progressives, or fits the religious agenda of faith-based mega-charity. No one funding what forms true community, real material resources and family stability. People here cruelly know the quiet grief felt around empty seats at Holiday tables, churches and schools, due to horrific endemic neighborhood violence and other *real* traumas—overdoses, alcoholism, mental-illness-infused violence, drug cartel extortion, gang shootings, early death due to cardiovascular disease, cancer, PFOFS, lead paint, asbestos, heavy metal poisoning, contaminated water, and other "acceptable doses" of community poisoning and divestment.

All this is reminiscent of Christopher Lasch's warnings in *Culture of Narcissism*[2], and its more dire companion describing social reordering and community rupture, *Revolt of the Elites*[3], both phenomenon widely observed and discussed from the 1980's "greed is good" philosophy, wealth reordering of the late 2000's, and new monopolization of capital and companies since the dot.com bust, COVID-19 pandemic, and whatever will follow the Obama, Biden and Trump eras, each applying their own "fix" to America. Regardless of who is in the White House, these aforementioned very real and persistent elements of regular people's lives are reminiscent of Eddie Murphy's subtly dark and satirical "Mr. Robinson's Neighborhood" skits on *Saturday Night Live*, as well as other comedy and music from that era. Luther Vandross's *With a Christmas Heart* and *Give Love on Christmas Day*, Boyz II Men's *Why Christmas*, and David Foster and Natalie Cole's *Grown up Christmas List* all echo the human spirit seeking reprieve from senseless suffering, isolation from neighbor and kin, and guidance for how to preserve our light in the dark nights of the soul[4, 5, 6, 7, 8, 9] and darkest time of the year. It was music like this and community realities around me that formed a strong part of the foundation for my progressive conservatism, and conservative yet progressive values.

The Soul Abhors a Vacuum

If we're being honest, outside of Black/African-American musicians, there was not much innovation in soul-stirring Holiday music, stylistics or interpretation regarding Christmas/holiday music between the 1950s and 1990s. At least, little from those eras is *strongly* held in current popular consciousness. In preparation for this book's release, I polled my diverse (age, ethnicity, income, religion) patient groups, which confirmed this opinion. An exception many of us can vaguely remember are those *non-cannon* music, downloaded from some old workplace or corporate chain playlist, on repeat from Thanksgiving to Christmas. The Walgreens pharmacy playlist is permanently archived in my brain. These playlists were vague suggestions of music, but mostly Muzak (aka. "elevator music"). Or perhaps you remember echoes of a shopping mall's lame attempt at curating a playlist of "multicultural" holiday music. I would term these payola tracks the (poorly attempted, and worse-interpreted) "affirmative action mix"—

---

one R&B singer, two boy bands crooning (ethnicity and sexual orientation rotates), one adolescent diary pop star jingle (hair color rotating), two dance/Disco/Hip-Hop covers of actual Christmas classics, two universally agreeable Christmas classics, one pop-Country star, and *Feliz Navidad*—a "perfect ten". But not crowd pleasers, and without intending so, contributing to several generations' jadedness about multicultural appreciation, the Winter Holidays and related traditions eventually becoming stereotypes of themselves, an ironic meta-mix.

Ultimately, playlists and sales-driven music like this fail to form any strong multi-cultural *appreciation*, necessary for stable and thriving community, a steadfast mutually agreeable goal of pro- gressives *and* conservatives. Speaking of *Feliz Navidad*, the track is an important and notable *exception* to the previous denunciation. This Latin/Hispanic song remains widely popular because the piece simply captures the soulful well-wishes and blessings of holiday gatherings among friends and family. Written by the Grammy winning José Feliciano, a Puerto Rican, it was also easy for the general public to embrace and adopt as new "American" Holiday/ Christmas song cannon. Another notable concession should be given to Native American pop singer, Jana Mashonee (Lumbee Nation, North Carolina; Tuscarora Nation, New York) who was invited to perform for President Obama and First Lady Laura Bush. Mashonee's Christmas album comprises traditional cannon (Jana is Christian), but uniquely sung in ten distinct indigenous North American languages, including Lumbee and Cherokee. Also an exception, the widely popular Bobby Vinton, "The Polish Prince" of American pop, who *unashamedly* wove Polish/Lithuanian culture into his songs, creating a quality and lasting woolen throw of warming popular Christmas/ Holiday music. Vinton's *Dearest Santa* and *Christmas Prayer* echoes themes of the "lean months" from the perspective of an orphan, albeit less gritty than his Black counterparts.

But most of the "new music" would not have made the average person's Jeopardy, Wheel of Fortune or Family Feud, or pub trivia category quiz knowledge. Nor would they have been easily summoned during a Tonight Show/Late Show street interview. We have been *long- overdue* for a fresh infusion of *soul* and *new stories* into our holiday Americana music and our inherited Christmas/Hanukkah classics. Musicologists like Dr. Arianne Honnold tell us fresh holiday and Christmas music is written every time a new genre or style emerges on the popular music scene. This is true of Hanukkah music and comedy also, courtesy of more writers and comedians pursuing the craft than Adam Sandler. But not every musical genre or style can write a *memorable, soulful or archetypally-relevant* Christmas or holiday song.

If it does not have deep archetypal resonance, it will not stay in the peoples' affections and memory beyond the moment, fad or hype of the current musical genre's era. When it is no longer pop, it will fade from memory.

Physicist and psychologist, Marie-Louise von Franz says "A symbol really lives only when it is the best and highest expression for something divined but not yet known to the observer. It then compels his [her] unconscious participation and has a life-giving and life-enhancing effect....[and opposites are] united in the symbol."[10] As Latin music has gained mass-popularity and respect across the United States—paralleling Hispanic and Latino culture becoming a mainstay of America—popular artists have emerged like the José Feliciano and Mariah Carey to write and perform new Christmas/holiday cannon music. Carey's loved/hated song, *All I want for Christmas is You* is still going strong, thirty years on, as is *Feliz Navidad*. While many songs have subcultural appeal, they are bound mostly to the affections and musical taste of a specific generation, niche, clique, or countercultural group.

Comedy or Cruelly Sacrilegious?

Much of the criticism I hear in my clinical office about the Winter Holidays is to a degree very fairly warranted. But not their cynicism. Not the habitual and ritualized complaint sessions. Nor the biting and unwavering poorly-considered attitudes, "I want you to agree with me—totally and affirmably—and my misery, my jaded principles, and my perpetually emotionally wounded guile."

There needs to be room for the Trickster's irony, amusing coincidences and paradoxes that are naturally occurring in the world and human condition. Yet instead, what we have seen over the last fifty-years, and what we do see today, is many artists, comedians, content creators and critics profaning something they don't *really* understand. To mock, troll and dump-on traditions you were not raised in, have not practiced yourself, and are only peripherally "educated" about, is basically dishonest. Your scornful critique is shallow. Your contempt is often shadow boxing with your own head.

Instead of seeking the good in the traditions, amplifying them and using that as the foundation for reforms and improvement, such people almost glee for cultural scorched-earth situations. Which as students of history, we recognize as a very Soviet approach to "progress", and "enlightened" cultural revolutions. The end result is not much different than what religious zealotry and militant theocracies historically create. Both forms are and have been very much derided by the same Soviet and Communist fanboys and cheerleaders. Now who is making the joke?

Other attempts at new Christmas/holiday music are often

---

wastefully no more than crude satire, usually a "race to the bottom". This variety of shock comedy is intentionally, obtusely vulgar, heavily sardonic, using debasing and gleefully sacrilegious statements, more than actually being universally funny. Rarely does this types of humor resound tales of life's natural situational comedy/tragedy dance, abundant in the human condition. One of the strong exceptions, a song which performs a typical Holiday situation with Celtic cultural *craic*—i.e. riotously amusing storytelling and physical humor—is The Irish Rovers' *Miss. Fogarty's Christmas Cake*. This pub-style song exaggerates the humorous and socially frustrating effects of *terrible* food foisted upon guests.

Sadly, most Christmas "comedy" songs rarely contains any type of *quality* witty satire, or savvy and *appropriately* earned trickster/paradoxical observation of Holiday excess—consumerism, binging alcohol/drugs/food, manic pantomimes of "spirit"—or a well-deserved roasting commercialization at one end, and the overly-pious pseudo-religiosity on the other end. This type of Christmas comedy is also often passive-aggressive, offering no workable pathway forward. It fails to teach, ultimately composing an awkward emotional or intellectual rant. In sharp contrast, this poetry collection is about finding a new harmony, one that honors traditions, recognizes "soul-capital" and symbolic richness, and innovates with the *zeitgeist* or rejuvenating "spirit of the times", but does not hold back on irony and critique. The British singer, Greg Lake's, *I Believe in Father Christmas* (Lake, Sinfield, Prokofeiff, 1977) challenges us to strongly confront that (possibly appropriate experiential cynicism), while recognizing our sense of wonder, whimsey and magic also has to mature beyond childhood's "magical thinking", so the Winter Holidays can feed our souls and spirit and bodies again. Many poems in this collection speak directly to this modern tension. It is crucial for the health of ourselves, our families and communities that we challenge ourselves with these choices, and not succumb to adolescent/juvenile psychological false liberations.

Jazz Resurrections

The first serious attempt that I can recall at resurrecting some of this Jazz-era music for new generations (older Boomers, Gen-X, Millennials, Gen-Z), as well as writing *new* Christmas songs in that vintage Big Band style, was the Brian Setzer Orchestra and Big Bad Voodoo Daddy. Both American rockabilly, jazz and big band swing fusion groups have lasted, and thrived, long past the "Neo-swing Revival" and Ska craze of the 1990s. These groups blend three to four styles of uniquely American music, also writing and performing their original songs of American classic car culture, the juiced-up covers of the Big Band Jazz era's top hits, and the bluegrass and Rockabilly/ Rock and Roll scene that burst Chuck Berry, Link Wray, Big Momma Thorton, Elvis and numerous other nearly-forgotten guitar and performance virtuosos. Many of us around Flint and Detroit residents and expats descended from "Rosie Riveter" and Women's Army Corps (WAC, WAAC) and Women's Airforce Service Pilots (WASP) grand-mothers, Arsenal of Democracy machinist grandfathers, and other relatives that fought and died in World War II. The neo-swing revival of the 1990s-2000s helped bridge these generations, and was noted in popular journalism of the time.

Like many of my Midwest and Rust Belt cohort, I was raised on the Christmas Top 40 classics, but also had the pleasure soothing my tinnitus addled ears with Motown and R&B. Napster, LimeWire, Gnutella and iTunes were still new and inaccessible to most of us, so variety and exposure was limited to my school teachers, professors, neighbors, friend's parents, and my own radio and record store curiosity. Both sets of my grandparents were from the World War II generation, so our holidays subsisted off a *dense* musical fruitcake of Jazz Big Bands albums, Andy Williams, Sinatra, Dean Martin and other crooners. As elders inevitably, often begrudgingly, yield control of the kitchen and stereo to the youth, my parents and aunts and uncles occasionally managed to add Manheim Steamroller, Charlie Brown/ Peanuts, The Beach Boys, Louis Armstrong, B.B. King, and of course Nat King Cole. Being classically and jazz trained on alto sax, most of this music was a soul food agreeable to my palate. My love of Delta and Chicago Blues, Zydeco and bluegrass taught me psychology before any formal training, and in many situations, it remains a superior diagnostic and treatment tool.

Polish Freedom Music

Most Poles who immigrated to America, Canada and Western Europe since the Cold War will bluntly express their unfavorable opinions of their direct experience with Soviet style Socialism and Communism, its Edenic illusions and integrity-lacking Total State tyranny, and how that system *truly* oppresses the soul and human spirit. Also their horror, confusion, and at times disgust, for the naivety widespread among America's youth (1960s and today) who appear to "drool" for Communism, via a false nostalgia for that which they have never known, and influenced by an unthoroughly examined Edenic psychological projection of Socialist utopia. Even after the Polish Solidarity Movement (aka. *Solidarność*) of the Gdansk dock workers and their other labor unions helped push aside the Iron Curtain, American education (outside Polish cultural meccas of Michigan, Indiana, Chicago, Buffalo, NYC, Pittsburg) still largely doesn't teach much, if any, Polish or Eastern European history.

Those Solidarity members were a major force in ending the Cold War, and the reasons and methods behind their movement and victory over the oppression of the Soviet system is essential for understanding the 20th and shaping 21st Centuries. Their defiance of soul-crushing Communist atheism (where the State is god, and Party propaganda is gospel), was greatly sustained their traditional practice of Christian holidays and festivals (including Christmas). These traditional holidays are interwoven and inseparable from Polish folk culture, so also provided the Polish people's and society's soul and spirit recovery from the horrors of the 20th Century—WWI, Polish-Soviet War, WWII, the Holocaust, Stalin's purges, and Martial Law. Polish Nobel Laureate, Wislawa Szymborska—a poet who participated in and lived through most of these events—writes in *The Turn of the Century*[11]

"It was supposed to be better than the rest, our twentieth
    century,
But it won't have time to prove it.

Already too much has happened
That was not supposed to happen

Stupidity is not funny,
Wisdom is not cheerful.

There are not questions more urgent
Than the naïve ones."

A major theme in the Christmas story is faith (Mary's "yes", Joseph's loyal fidelity and protection). Faith often begins with the Fool Archetype's presence which is a state of not-knowing, innocent ignorance, curiosity, being embolden with the "heart of discovery", or naivety. Like Frodo's agreement to take the journey to Mordor in Lord of the Rings. Allowing the spirit of Christmas to renew us requires starting with what the Taoists and Buddhists call the "beginner's mind", combining with what the Sufi poets (Rumi, Hafiz, Mirabai, Kabir, Saadi) call the winged heart.

In Sufiism, the ecstatic (winged) heart is a core symbol—resembling the winged heart imagery of American Rock and Roll (borrowed from the ancient Persians and Sufiism)—and similar to the Ancient Greeks' concept of *dithyramb* and *agape*[12]. For Greek pagans this was/is a tribute to Dionysus, and for Greek Christians, the inherited style is closer to what modern people would call "worship poetry", hymns, trance/ rhythmic group performance poetry, or even modern psalms and private worship. In these interpretations, the psychological energy of the ecstatic heart is also similar to the Greek concept and experience of *agape*, or love for the divine, the transpersonal, the transcendent. In popular culture, most non-religious people would know the winged heart imagery of American Rock and Roll (inspired by Sufiism and ancient Persian symbols), hence why many of the poems in this collection are infused with influence from Sufi poetry.

We say "yes" to the journey before we know the complete path or destination. No lesser, was such influence of the Poles' Christian hymns on themselves and their country. Like freedom songs of Black American slaves during the Antebellum South, and after Emancipation during the Jim Crow era, the Poles sang during their pilgrimages and marches around Poland. And slowly, sonically aided, fractured the Berlin Wall's enharmonic rebar, a somber structure which was a monument to the actual censorship of otherwise *real* proletariat culture (live and let live).

Everyday People, Workers Music, and Unromantic Rural America

Another notable *exception* to the Christmas creative stagnation is the American Country and Bluegrass music scenes, which produced some new original hits during the early 2000s in 2010s. This music's themes followed the tenor of the aforementioned Black American music—struggle, poverty, pride in self, family, community concern. Some became strongly patriotically infused, and included veterans' and their families' experiences following September 11, 2001 and escalation of the Global War on Terror—deployment depression, fear, PTSD, loss of a parent.

With the birth of social media, and sharing of all the new (and old) music globally on the Internet, many up-and-coming musicians, church groups, hidden away mountain musicians of Appalachia, and local bar bands of hidden talent tried their hand at some new and unique songwriting. Homemade music videos demonstrating authentic alternatives to Hallmark, harlequin romance cover art, and MTV/VH1 also enhanced the new music's appeal. Currently, a strong European folk revival is thriving, especially in the former Soviet states. Especially toward rejuvenating medieval "peasant" music, as it was called prior to the premodern era. This has reinvigorated the Celtic, Germanic, and Slavic, Arabic, Native American/Canadian First Nations, and Jewish Music scenes quite strongly, and restored to global knowledge, a large part of our musical human heritage. Often, they are blended with world music and popular styles. Some notable groups—Maria Pomianowska (Poland), Julie Fowlis (Scotland), Hrdza (Czech Republic/Slovakia), Yair Dalal (Israel), DakhaBrakha

(Ukraine), Light in Babylon (Turkey, Iran), Warsaw Village Band (Poland), Yamma Ensemble (Israel), Laboratorium Piesni (Poland), Loreena McKennitt (Canada), Carlos Nakai (Navajo, Ute), Joglaresa w/ Belinda Sykes (United Kingdom), Sutari (Poland), Shelley Morningsong (Northern Cheyanne), Trio Mandili (Republic of Georgia), Rokiczanka (Poland). Similar movements are happening in Africa, Russia, and the broader Indian subcontinent.

Through the "radio" receiver of my second clinical and academic field, Depth Psychology, (Social Work was the first) we would receive these global cultural waves as the resonance of the *Puer* (divine child, newness, spontaneity) and the *Senex* (wise elder, tradition, consistency) Archetypes[10, 13, 14] at work. In the past decade, it feels rare to hear Americans and American institutions working with these two archetypes *harmonically*—revitalizing the old, while respecting the new, tuning an alchemical fusion that actually sustains and births new culture and traditions. We Americans would be wise to note how this this sonic congruence of our voices is achieved, and how learning of how these mingled archetypal perspectives could assist fine-tuning our increasingly divisive and radically polarized American society into a mutually beneficial, polyphonic composition. New American songs, by the people, for the people.

The past decades' stagnation and creativity was not only an American phenomenon. Perhaps greatly accounted for by the deep wounds of two World Wars, colonialism's rise and fall, the Soviet occupation of Eurasia, and expansion of religious-based terrorism between the 1960s and present day. As I conducted research for this book and my clinic's annual winter holidays music and film collage, a continued challenge I encounter is finding foreign language covers of American holiday music recorded with *rich soulfulness*. It's one of the places the Atlantic cultural disconnect is immediately noticeable.

The Europeans don't seem to really understand "American" Christmas music, except in pantomime. We have forgotten and lost connection with the spirit of our European heritage, the Mediterranean, the Indian subcontinent, and Africa, and Asia. Similarly, Americans always love a coffee break, but don't understand Scandinavian *Fika*, a coffee tradition more like British tea. Russians understand the cold, and the winter probably more than anyone, except Inuits. But they don't appear to love and celebrate it like Canadians, Scandinavians, Alaskans, Rocky and Sierra Mountain natives, New Englanders and upper Midwest Americans do. For Russian's, there's is almost a lament and dread of winter. But what should we expect from a culture that partially descended from Mediterranean people, the Byzantine's, hailing from lands where the sun always shined? And no one really understands Israel, but has an armchair opinion. The real work is done through people like Yair Dalal[15], a famous Iraqi-Jewish musician (of oud and violin). He adeptly blends Arab, Jewish and Western Classical music in a form which sings sweetly and hauntingly dark to both Eastern and Western audiences, religious and non-religious people. Dalal's musical mission has been recognized for providing peacemaking and cultural understanding, especially between Arabs and Jews in Israel and the broader Middle East. The arts, especially through music, will continue to be an approachable and productive neutral ground for cultural *appreciation* and peacemaking (as they always have been), in the best genial spirit of international brother and sisterhood.

Christmas as Spiritual and Secular Community in Times of Fracture

It is in the history of Christmas, the songs and hymns, that tells the story of Christianity, the Church but also most of Western Civilization that we know. For us modern people, inheritors of complicated legacies, wrestling with the paradoxes, scandals, controversies, the salvation of mother church and its fellowship community, and those who have left religious practice due to these scandals, moral/ethical paradoxes, and actual prejudice—may, perhaps, start to be found in the songs and the stories of Christmas. For I believe the music records the best spirit of Christianity and the "meaning of Christmas". This book seeks to demonstrate and point to *some* examples and methods of recovering the Winter Holidays' "gold" from the "shadow". The Shadow and "shadow work" are both currently trending in psychology, self-help and online self-improvement circles, but very old Depth Psychology concept and model, which C.G. Jung translated from Medieval Alchemical texts that surrounds these traditions. This poetry collection is also intended as a topical beginners guide for examining our personal and cultural "shadow" and Psychological Complexes (Jung, Johnson, Moore, Shalit, Weller)[4, 5, 8, 16, 17] that surround traditions, celebration, being on holiday, engaging in meaningful symbolic enactment, rituals and rites.

To "live everyday like Christmas" is not simply a Feeling resonance in the heart, or outward sense of charity. It *is not* indiscriminate receptivity to everything and anything our Ego's hedonism/power craves, nor what others tell us is proper to think/feel, and we absentmindedly socially rehearse. "Living like Christmas" essentially requires connecting with presence of *mature* Archetypal Feminine and *mature* Archetypal Masculine[13, 14, 18, 19, 21, 22]—both terms which are about symbolizing ways of being and vital character development components, not gender. Ritual is the container, spirit the intention and soul is the energy that fuels it. There is no Christmas story without the Archetypal Feminine, exemplified in Queen form by the Madonna[8] (aka. Mary, Maryam, Miriam), mother of Christ/Jesus, who needs to explanation or introduction. But also, all the women (and Archetypal Feminine presence and forms) that supported birthing the "new light".

In the Bible stories' examples, the primary supporters include, but are not limited to the following. Anne (mother of Mary, wife of Joachim), providing elder's/cronehood blessings, hope and inspiration and blessing of potential (i.e. Bible story of the Presentation at the Temple). Next is Elizabeth, a wise peer and family friend. She is a woman possessing long life practical experiences, loyal family kinship, learned patience and gratitude for long-differed dreams (one example being waiting for children as she aged, and the pains of decades of infertility). Not least, but often not fully appreciated or recognized, the nameless midwives, people who likely and pragmatically would have been called-in to be present at Jesus's birth. Or as is still custom in Hebrew tradition (and among modern people) in the immediate aftermath/recovery period. They represent wisdom of the body, medicine, restoration of physical health after ordeals and imitations (spiritual or physical). Later significant supports include but at not limited to, Mary Magdalene, and the sisters Mary and Martha. Peer community supports, friendship, love, those who carry on our work in their own manner, and people inspired by our creativity, and "birth" their own, continuing the cycle.

There also is no Christmas story or birthing the new light without the Archetypal Masculine[13, 14, 18, 19, 21, 22], exemplified in Christ as the King[8]. In the Bible stories, masculine supporters included Joseph (step-father, guardian, loyal surrogate and relatable fathering). Also the Three Wise Men, kings and alchemists/Magi—Melchior, Gaspar, Balthasar), all with additional knowledge and philosophical perspectives. The many shepherds, people with practical knowledge about the land, resources, the animal world, and self-care and independence skills outside of official institutions (the village/society), etc. Finally, Joachim, affirming value and inspiring confidence in the potential (via his visionary prophecy). And there is no Christmas story without community. "Living like Christmas" is not merely confined to conducting our actions with other-love and a personal generative social attitude, both which are forms of embodying Archetypal Mature Masculinity[19, 20, 21, 22, 23, 24]. Mature Masculinity is importantly distinct from "power-archy" (Marion Woodman), or what progressives and feminists call "toxic masculinity".

If we are going to take integrating the Archetypes of Christmas seriously, it also requires ecumenical renewal and eschatological inspiration utilizing the powerful symbolism and presence of the Holy

Spirit in us all. C.G. Jung believed the Holy Spirit [Ghost] was not just one archetype among multitudes, but may be *the essence of all archetypes and archetypal experiences*[25]. This assertion echoes Plato's "essential forms" of all creation, also what George Lucas based the Star Wars "Force" phenomenon upon, and von Franz (2004) work on the one world, *unus Mundus*, of which both psyche and matter are two expressions of that one essence. Participating in the physical forms Christmas decorations and ritual has a renewal of the psyche effects connecting people to the spirit of the seasons traditions. The psychological impact of poetry and songs that bring a soulful awareness of the winter and her meaning, aids people in being able to feel physically better in the snowy, cold, dark months. This collection widely and deeply explores this phenomenology through our inherited Winter Holidays' traditions.

In the secular universalist sense, the Holy Spirit could also be understood and experienced as "brotherhood/ sisterhood" or the "heart of humanity". In adopting such an attitude, intellectual perspective, behavior, or informing our faith with this assertion does *not* mean, we become ideal Christians, Born Again, reverts, New Age spiritualists, "woke", ex-religious, "fully liberated nones", "recovered" from religion, atheists, Gnostics, or agnostic. It does, for myself and others, bring to mind the theologian Paul Tillich's existential question, "what is your ultimate concern?"[26] If you don't have a god, then what have you made into your god, and how do you worship it?

Your answer will greatly influence how you experience and practice (or don't) the Winter Holidays. Your answer will echo the (perhaps hidden) mantra your chant in yourself while you move through life, relate to other human beings, and understand the large (or small) story you are living. It The idea of "epic" and rich living, large or small, is not a sardonic or cynically ironic joke, but actually an achievable part of our humanity, even if for many it only occurs in short small fleeting moments. As Erving Polster said in his book of the same title, "every person's life is worth a novel."[26] Many of us simply do not look for, or more common these days with the loss of elders, mentors and adulthood initiation[17, 18 19 20, 21, 22, 28] *have not been shown how* to translate the sheet music of our still-being-composed rock-opera, or opus symphony into a language we understand, or a storyline we recognize when it plays through the stereo in our head.

This poetry collection's story arc begins with late-Autumn American Midwest (and Canadian) hunting season, an annual event that marks for many families, the beginning of the secular "Holidays", American Thanksgiving, the Christmas season (Advent), Winter Solstice, possibly Hanukkah, and the natural transformation to the Winter season. Traditionally, the Whitetail Deer, and less frequently other "stags"—Antelope, Elk, Axis Deer, Moose, etc.—are harvested for the Christmas table. It remains common to purchase extra harvest tags from the local State wildlife regulation agency and give another struggling family the meat, or donate to a shelter. Our North American traditions echo the annual practice of fattening of the Christmas goose or other domesticated or the family hog, wild boar hunting, or pheasant/grouse, or wild birds. Even if one is morally/ethically repulsed by meat-eating or animal harvesting, the essence of Jewish theologian, Martin Buber's "I and Thou"[28] principle applies to distribution of community resources, especially if available abundantly, and is essential to the Archetypes of Christmas and Hanukkah, the Winter Solstice feasts and the British/Celtic Revels. The spirit and social instruction and urging adherence to these historical practices is found the traditional Celtic/British song, *Christmas in the Old Man's Hat*. The "I and Thou" principle is especially important during our era, where the modern social norm (and ever- present social philosophy of the ego is increasingly "I and It"—hyper subjective perspectives and their projections, instead of real relationships[22, 27, 28, 29].

Dreadfully, there is an even darker version, which has always been part of the human condition. It is the philosophy and worldview of dictators, oligarchy, and other exploiters and those with evil-corrupted souls—hoarding wealth, food, tools for work, and other resources essential for basic human needs. Why? While taking a pass on all other forms of being and relates in this world, they intentionally create artificial dependency, unnecessary hardship (not the natural type that is part of aging, maturation, learning, skills building and character development). They spread and amplify *meaningless suffering*— often part of a psychopathic sadistic pleasure or sociopathic boredom remedy—inflicted among those who have not, have no defenses, and area easily exploited. This is classical pure and *shameless pursuit of power* for the sake of power. Their ultimate concern? It is the deranged psychological desire to become a god.

Similarly, in the gritty common reality of winter poverty, and thinking of and elevating due respect to and desires for his fellow poets, writers, painters, and working people, poet Norman Williams shares his private thoughts in *A Christmas Song*,
"I think, that is, of others who
Withdrew from commerce and the world
To work for joy instead of gain.
O would that I could gather them
This Yuletide, and shower them with coins."[30]

Winter Solstice

Just as the empty space, and the pause and breath between notes and phrases resonates the most dynamic and interesting essence

37

of even a simple piece of music, so we need the empty and austere starkness of the Winter Solstice. Without retreat, we cannot hear the music of our souls. Without the breath, we are artificially tense, paused frozen and cannot feel the spirit, nor discern it from our ego's mental chatter and *id's* drives. We need the archetypal dyad of the Solstice and Holiday/Christmas/Hanukkah, etc.—the extreme dark and the exemplary light of the tree, star, menorah and lanterns; the season's natural austere grey tones against celebrative color; minor keys and major keys, all reeling together in Chicago Polish church basement, Detroit's Saint Andrew's Hall, or around the Hanukkah table.

This book is also for people that call themselves "nones", the religiously, and more-often *spiritually* and existentially non-affiliated. Though I have found in my nearly twenty years of clinical experience, they often are *extremely* spiritually gifted, *but unmentored, undisciplined* and *un-honed.* "Nones" are also those who, in our fracturing times, find themselves existentially and psychologically drifting. They live a chaotic mélange of Dante's *Inferno*, Sartre's *No Exit*, Kafka's *Metamorphosis* and Dostoevsky's *Brothers Karamazov*. The collection's last poem brings us to an imagined music recording studio where pagans, Christians, modern secularists, existentialist philosophers, and Sufi poets have gathered to make and share musical soul food fusion.

Just as we have needed new holiday songs, so do we need new holiday poems. In the spirit of Christmas and Hanukkah, this collection is my contribution to our public archetypal gift table. These poems, prose and stories are, as C.S. Lewis notes of Father Christmas's gifts, "tools, not toys". I interpret Lewis's narrative shift from secular or religious Christmas (and Hanukkah by proxy) being a ritual of excess and even debauchery, to a holiday season of harmonic paradoxes. The curious appearance of the archetypal figure, Father Christmas, in C.S. Lewis's *The Lion, The Witch, and The Wardrobe* demonstrates that the Winter Holidays (especially Christmas) are mutually and paradoxically a time for joy *and* solemnity, and *also* elevating (extroverted) celebration *and* deep private (introverted) contemplation. Modern Winter Solstice celebrations, and New Year's holiday could be this, but often degrade into carnival, debauchery, and regrettable decisions, which C.S. Lewis called the excess of Exmas. Regarding the more balanced and intentional celebration and contemplation, my field of Depth Psychology refers to this as "spirit and soul work" (Hillman)[13], an extension of C.G. Jung's "shadow work"[1, 5, 7, 8, 9, 17, 30]. Dr. Jankowski further said, "Without these archetypes, all knowledge remains distant and unrelated to one's lived experiences". For an extremely thorough examination of Depth Psychology's spirit and soul work for modern people and society, presented in a scientific and spiritual but not religious context, see Dr. Vanessa Jankowski's work, *Modern Challenges of Consciousness According to Jung, Hillman, von Franz, and Woodman.*[23]

This collection has emerged during the past decade or so of great chaos in American culture, politics, and spirit, but this book is not only for Americans. *Unorthodox* is a threshold handshake, and invitation to a living room concert. It is offered to people of my generation, those a bit older, and those seven generations who will follow us, inheriting our choices and legacies.[31] You may be feeling the lingering crushing isolation of social anomie, nihilism, dread or disgust at the absurd and painful missed-potential of our resources, our nation, and the human spirit. The following patiently, joyfully, and at times painfully crafted poetry and prose, were written especially for those living without a sense of story, those who do not know what myth—whether it be Divine, agnostic, or atheist—they understand themselves enacting.

Paradoxically, we also live in an *exciting* time, because new music focused on our collective heritage, traditions and rituals, holidays and winter celebrations are being written, produced and actually becoming known on the public airwaves and curated on private playlists. I don't have any expectations or aspirations these poems will become the lyrics of new holiday songs, plots for future plays in Chicago's Theater District, New York's Broadway, London, Toronto, settings for a future "classic" Christmas films, or inspire modern dance choreography for fusion styles common to L.A., Berlin, Gdansk. Or traditional revival in Detroit, Kiev, Tbilisi, Kerela, Moscow, Budapest, Istanbul, Beirut, Addis Ababa, Cairo. However, this collection is gifted to you in that spirit, and I hope you will find them thought provoking, deep feeling, sensationally stimulating, and spiritually stirring. My best wishes are that the poems within will help to replace cheap sentimentality and fleeting nostalgia, with soulful fertilizer for the towering "evergreens" which anchor your family, home and community, and shelter and feed travelers guests and pilgrims from other communities that seek cultural parley, so we may *all* better benefit from continuing the best of our American Experiment. Peace be with you all. *Na Zdrowie!*

References:
1. "The problem of opposites called up by the shadow plays a great—indeed, the decisive—role in alchemy, since it leads in the ultimate phase of the work to the union of opposites in the archetypal form of the hieros gamos [hierogamy, or holy/sacred] marriage}, or "chymical wedding." Here the supreme opposites, male and female (as in the Chinese yang and yin), are melted into a unity purified of all opposition and therefore incorruptible."

Jung, Carl G. Collected Works, vol 12, 37. Princeton University Press. Princeton, NJ.

2. Lasch, Christopher (1991). Culture of Narcissism: American Life in an Age of Diminishing Expectations. W.W. Norton and Co. New York, NY.
3. Lasch, Christopher (1996). Revolt of the Elites and the Betrayal of Democracy. W.W. Norton and Co. New York, NY.
4. Johnson, Robert A. (2009). Owning Your Shadow. Harper. San Francisco, CA.
5. Johnson, Robert A. (2017). Inner Gold: Understanding Psychological Projection. Chiron Publications. Ashville, NC.
6. Saint John of the Cross. Dark Night of the Soul.
7. Moore, Thomas (2005). Dark Nights of the Soul: a Guide to Finding Your Way Through Life's Ordeals. Avery. New York, NY.
8. Moore, Thomas (2016). The Soul of Christmas. Franciscan Media. Cincinnati, OH.
9. Tarrant, John (1999). The Light Inside the Dark: Zen, Soul, and the Spiritual Life. Perrenial. New York, NY.
10. Von Franz, Marie-Louise (1995). Projection and Re-collection in Jungian Psychology. Open Court Books. pg.83. Chicago, IL.
11. Szymborska, Wislawa; Miłosz, Czeslaw; Trezciak, Joanna (trans.) (2002). Miracle Fair: Selected Poems of Wislawa Szymborska. W.W. Norton & Co. New York, NY.
12. A wildly (ecstatic) performed poem or hymn to the Divine. In polytheistic and pagan ancient Greece, this was often dedicated to Dionysus. Agape, a universal love, love for life, or love for/of the Divine.
13. Hillman, James; Slater, Glen (ed.) (2013). Senex and Puer. Uniform Edition of the Writings of James Hillman, vol. 3. Spring Publications. Putnam, CT. Harper. San Francisco, CA.
14. Von Franz, Marie-Louise (2000). The Problem of the Puer Aeternus. Inner City Books. Toronto, Canada.
15. Yair Dalal created "Zaman el Salaam", for the 1994 Nobel Peace Prize Ceremony for Yitzhak Rabin (who was assassinated for signing the Oslo Accords), Shimon Peres (Israeli PM), and Yasser Arafat (PLO Leader). Some prominent albums include Inshallah Shalom (2005), Band Orient (2008), Samar (1996).
16. Shalit, Erel (2002). The Complex: Path of Transformation from Archetype to Ego. Inner City Books. Toronto, Canada.
17. Weller, Francis (2015). The Wild Edge of Sorrow: Rituals of Renewal and the Sacred Work of Grief. North Atlantic Books. Berkeley, CA.
18. Moore, Robert; Gillette, Douglas (1990). King, Warrior, Magician, Lover: Rediscovering the Archetypes of the Mature Masculine. San Francisco, CA.
19. Moore, Robert; Gillette, Douglas (1992). The King Within: Accessing the King in the Male Psyche. William Morrow and Company/Harper Collins. New York, NY.
20. Bond, D. Stephanson (2003). The Archetype of Renewal: Psychological Reflections on Ageing, Death and the Rebirth of the King. Inner City Books. Toronto, Canada.
21. Johnson, Robert A. (1993). Transformation: Understanding the Three Stages of Masculine Consciousness. Harper One. San Francisco, CA.
22. Keen, Sam (1992). Fire in the Belly: On Being a Man. Bantam. New York, NY.

23. Jankowski, Vanessa (2024). Modern Challenges of Consciousness According to Jung, Hillman, von Franz, and Woodman. p. 137 (Publication No. 31560901) [Doctoral dissertation, Pacifica Graduate Institute]. ProQuest Dissertations Publishing. https://www.proquest.com/pqdtglobal1/dissertations-theses/modern-challenges-consciousness-according-jung/docview/3101097202/sem-2?accountid=45402 .

24. C.G. Jung. Collected Works vol. 9, Chapter 11, pg.85-86. "There is no doubt that his activities were founded on a numinous experience. Which is indeed characteristic of all those who are gripped by an archetype. This archetype is not of uniform meaning, but was originally an ambivalent dualistic figure that broke through again in the alchemical concept of spirit after engendering the most contradictory manifestations within the Holy Ghost movement itself...an espousal of the Holy Ghost in its Christian form should at the same time help the archetype of the spirt to break through in all its characteristic ambivalence."

25. Tillich, Paul; Church, F. Forester (ed.) (1988). The Essential Tillich: an Anthology of Writings of Paul Tillich. Collier. New York, NY.

26. Polster, Erving (1987). Every Person's Life is Worth a Novel. W.W. Norton. New York, NY.

27. Buber, Martin; Smith, Ronald Gregor (1937). I and Thou. T & T Clark. Edinburgh, Scotland.

28. Richo, David (2021). How to Be an Adult in Relationships: Five Keys to Mindful Loving. Shambhala. Boulder, CO.

29. Zweig, Connie; Wolf, Steve (1999). Romancing the Shadow: a Guide to Soul Work for a Vital, Authentic Life. Wellspring/Ballantine. Toronto, ON.

30. Williams, Norman (2003). "A Christmas Song", One Unblinking Eye. Swallow Press/Ohio University Press. Athens, OH.

*For a general introduction to my poetry and analysis/criticism, see Dr. Clifford Mayes's "The Poet as Archetypal Teacher in Unteachable Times: The Poetry of Kyle Jankowski", in New Visions and New Voices: Extending the Principles of Archetypal Pedagogy in Include a Variety of Venues, Issues, and Projects. Mayes, Clifford; Rinaldi, Jacquelyn (2023). Roman & Littlefield Publishers. Lanham, MD.

"The task of the modern educator is not to cut down jungles, but to irrigate deserts."

~C.S. Lewis

Considering Christmas in July
(Midsummer 2021)

A few years back, I remember mother's holiday card, *"I wonder if you even celebrate anymore."*

My table changes every year, with the guests, menu, music and décor, the hall of my home annually decked differently. Mostly, my wife and I stick to tree and trimmings. Sometimes more Slavic—ice maidens, evergreen wreathes, frost glazed berries and birch boughs. Celtic remembered also—bagpipes bellow *I Saw Three Ships*, Royal Stewart Christmas-esque tartan everywhere. Bobby Vinton taught me the spirit of Christmas in Killarney and that Santa is Polish. Other years, more the Midwestern and rural Christian simplicity, *à la* Joanna Gaines. Several times, I've decorated with Tim Allen (full-on American electric twinkle and tinsel). Regardless, *Wigilia's* wonder is always present.[1] Last year, I smiled as I braided boughs of ivy, discovered growing on my land among the cedar, hemlock, oak, ash and thorny black locust.[2]

Back at mother's home, the ceramic Dicken's Christmas village is reset into the same story, year after year. But unlike the Nativity birthing new life and joy within us, it's stuck in the well-known Rust-Belt nostalgia. Perhaps mother secretly painfully longing for Divine charity. Each year, unremittingly, is she trying to replicate the old downtown Flint Vogue's twelve window displays,[3] remembering the eight-story Smith-Bridgeman's[3] building bustling with holiday shoppers, filling the empty mantle shelves with her own brand of Christmas cheer?

She and I are both in agreement, no one in Flint (or the city herself) got a Fair deal.[3] We both await the sign, so Ebenezer Scrooge (my father, or hers?) may transform from emotional miser to full-hearted Christian. Or maybe she and the ex-pats wish for a long-vanished Flint[4]—a modern version of Victorian London's East End—to be merry and bright again.

But the ghosts of industrial past keep haunting the city.

1. Polish Christmas Eve celebration and customs.
2. *A Tree Song* by: Rudyard Kipling in his book "Puck of Pook's Hill" (1906).
3. Famous retail and departments stores of Flint, Michigan's heyday (1940s-1960s). themed sidewalk window dioramas and interior décor were similar to New York City's Macys and Chicago's Marshall Field's Christmas displays.
4. Edith Wharton speaks of "a long-vanished America" in her book *Age of Innocence.*

Sunrise on Opening Weekend

The three grown children, two with children of their own, tramp with their elderly father through the freshly frozen alfalfa field, with grass still poking through the white crust. Just enough to keep the deer coming back for another meal. Each hunter clad in blaze orange. Back in Chicago and Milwaukee, they would be mistaken for construction workers. Each is loaded down with a pack of essentials. Slung over everyone's shoulder are antique deer rifles, handed down through several generations, simple camp chairs, Swiss Army wool blankets, and their basic provisions. What's hunted here makes its way to everyone's Christmas table.

Today's lunch, ham and cheese sandwiches are leftovers from Thanksgiving, spiced with horseradish-mustard and mayonnaise on Italian. They each felt the cold-stiff granola bars with mixed nuts in their packs, after stepping out in the unseasonably bracing wind and blowing snow at 6:00 AM. The three also carrying extra salty oily chips and Hershey bars to keep the stomach furnace pumping. This is the rural Midwest after all, no need for gourmet delicatessen or exotic Chicago ingredients. One exception, Thermoses of hot pine nut coffee from Santa Fe, a treat and in-season. So why not?

At the trek's midway point, the group stops to rest at a line of haybales and give the old man a breather. In this perfect moment, we see the hay bales strewn about highlighted with a pink, orange, lavender and periwinkle sunrise, just peeking through the red, white and black oak tree line. Like modern sculptures or a Norman Rockwell painting.

Succor

O Sacred Bridal Chamber of the Word,[2]
The Flower of Incorruption...

Though we may seek His guidance in the Dark Night,
She first claims us, enfolding all in Her mantle
In times when all our small sacred things are profaned

By the perfect truth of untruth,

She faithfully blooms.

In the Bridal Chamber of the word,
We marry ourselves to Truth,
Holding close to our hearts,
The Flower of Incorruption.

1. "Succor" comes from two Latin words |sub – currere| meaning to 'to run beneath'. One who succors 'runs beneath ' someone who is falling. Succor, therefore, expresses exactly what a mother does when she sees her child falling, or hears it calling for help.
2. *Agni Parthene* (Greek: O Virgin Pure"), and Orthodox Christian/Byzantine Prayer to the Theotokos (Mary), composed by St. Nectarios of Aegina (1905).

Advent Wreath
(November 28, 2021)

"And looking at those sitting in a circle round him, he said 'Here are my mother and my brothers. Anyone who does the will of God, that person is my brother and sister and mother.'" (Mark 3:34-35 - NJB)

The Advent Wreath,

Like an icon
Suffuses mind and heart,
Helping us see through the Solstice's darkness visible,[1]

Find those who have no circles of kinship,
Embracing them in the light of the wreath.
As we welcome to the table
Both those going nowhere and those with nowhere to go.

You welcome us all into this place.

After so much tumult, plague,

This year Hanukkah and Advent align.

Sunday,
As I see the wreath's first candle lit in the sanctuary,
Across the desert
My adoptive Hebrew mother lights the Menorah's first candle.

Hanukkah,
Remembering endurance and great trials.

Matka Boża,
Your great journey and trial began here.
Love alighting in each belabored step.
When all energy has left our bodies, You show us

The just flame gathers us
Into circles of truth.

1. Milton, *Paradise Lost.* Book 1, Line 63.
2. Polish: "Mother of God".

Hunting
(Wisconsin, December)

I sit in a stand with my Scottish-American and Cherokee father-in-law. Both of us clad in blaze jackets and bibs (not kilt), camo fleece, the long johns everyone gets for Christmas at some point, Gore-Tex gloves and duck boots from Maine. Half a century ago, his father-in-law would have donned Pendleton red buffalo plaid, a folding fleece ear hat from Wisconsin, Red Wing work boots (straight from a long week building fireplaces), and surplus wool G.I. gloves. Those days ended when someone realized a lot of hunters are red/green color blind. Today we are hunting stag. Our blind and camp chairs are mossy oak patterned, like these Midwest woodlands enveloping us with their peely paper birch, black oaks, blackjacks and towering maples. We sit among rolling Wisconsin dells. No amusement park here. This is serious business. My first hunt. After six hours of still observation but not one sighting, my father-in-law ventures from our perch to tramp through the hills and gullies. He the master hunter has gone out into the tangle of hardwoods and bramble, aiming to flush any bedded-down whitetails my way. I remain in the aged, weathered, but sturdy, pine and plywood tower he built in his 60s. Hauled overland, built board by board on site. I wait in the early winter silence, clutching his father-in-law's 30-06 Browning semi auto, like I'm on fire watch. My focus drops for a moment to the scrollwork engraved near the walnut fore stock. I remember his father-in-law's uncles all served in the Great War, and briefly wonder if this is one of those civilian converted decommissioned BARs or the newly smithed peacetime Safari model. Only the squirrels scampering around break the silence, as they enjoy collecting a dinner of sweet Chinkapin Oak acorns, rustling through a forest carpet, a peaceful sound as familiar to my father-in-law as it was to the nearby Ho-Chunk tribe's ancestors, or the French missionaries and fur trappers once ranging down from Canada. In the silence I sit, at the crossroads of time.

"The inner man has to be fed — a fact that moderns, with their frivolous trust in reason, often overlook to their own harm."

-Carl G. Jung

Swipes
(early December)

Assembling myself on a curb-facing, unassuming café's lunch counter stool, nestled in a trendy and youthful Chicago neighborhood, I lunch. I like this Greek family's food and management, and most patrons and the cooks—we each still have the decency to avoid politics, and just get the coffee and gyros and kebabs and baklava and the check. Outside, families and some youth brave the Chicago chill for early holiday boutique shopping. I see my Greek chai coffee's complex aroma mirrored, by the strolling friends and lovers. Some arm in arm, heartily laughing, talking care-free. With their walking meditations, and cross-stitched-cultural-conversations, some are unknowingly repairing their inherited lacerated and slashed family tapestries.

The Fates may clear the carefully strategized chessboard of your life with a swipe of their hands, just as swiping your finger orients your fate, and another's, toward the same stage. Comedy or tragedy, drama is assured. Fate's tapestry is woven with delicate threads. Not a useful shield against Roman knives, or as camouflage cloak, when silver pieces are distributed among your circles. Rather than swiping *hard,* right or left, they are working their curious fingers across the Creator's loom, learning to deftly navigate create, illustrate a new story, between the worn guidelines.

*Internet-based dating has reduced the soul and interpersonal kinship experiences of dating to a reductionistic sense perception of the eyes, arousal response and sexual glands. Yet, the techno-dystopian age has not yet robbed us of all. The Fates still intervene, and people of promising kinship and love find one another.

Stella Maris
(2nd Sunday of Advent 2020)

And her eyes were dark and holy
Blue flames in the inky night.

1. *Stella Maris* (Latin: "Star of the Sea"), a veneration of the biblical Mary, Mother of Jesus. *Ave Maris Stella* (Latin: "Hail, star of the sea) is an eighth century Marian hymn used at Vespers (evening prayers). A major theme of this song is Mary's ability to loosen the chains of guilt.

Wassailing

"Born among miracles reported from two thousand years ago, it cannot expect to impress that sturdy common sense which can withstand the plainest and most palpable evidence for miracles happening at this moment."
– G.K. Chesterton

Snowless bitter brown early December.
Not much yet carries the light of Christmas.

Suddenly, I feel called to walk and wassail through my land, in the
    old way.
Past the English Ivy, cutting a few yards for the fireplace mantle.
Through the wild rose archway, collecting rosehips for tonight's hot
    tea,
Leaving enough so the drab landscape flashes occasionally
With cardinals' blue jays' and gold finches'
Feathers coloring the community by day, the neighbors' twinkle
    lights by night.

Down the rise I trod into the savannah forest,
Weaving the raspberry trellises,
Which at a glance resemble worn Royal Stewart Tartans. I remember
    the Queen, pause for a prayer.
Humming around the black cherry, white oak, black walnuts,
    cranberry, redbuds and spice bush.
Marveling the buckeyes, wondering if they roast like chestnuts.
Circling the linden, the king's tree, staring skyward.
Stepping among the seven white-spire birches,

Glowing crowns against the not-yet-frozen mire.

—

Saint Nicholas Day in Old Scotland
(to Father Gerard Manley Hopkins)

"He's the slave of all slaves who serve's none but himself." – Scottish Proverb

Woolen socks hung by the hearths
With kilts coats and cloaks
Hebrides tweeds
Ancient tartans
Aristocratic-reaching argyle
Simple homespun fleck and provincial plaid styles,
Each regal in its own way.

Thawing frozen feelings slush from the homeward trudge,
And too many neighbors' cold countenance.

The families fortunate enough to have everyone annually freshly
cobbled,
Among the lucky few in the lowlands to have had
A generous-hearted lady and laird,
Especially at Christmas,
Fancied themselves Saints Brigid or Nicholas[1]
Leaving essentials and treats for the tenant families upon the clan's
land.

Awaiting inside stockings boots brogues and ghillies lined up near
the warm hearth's fieldstone,
Rock candy, sweet shortbread, butterscotch for the children,
Tack and trades' tools for father,
Wool and books and tonics for mother.
Mandarins all the way from China and lemons from Spain.
Laird and baron had been to sea and on campaign.
Both knew scurvy's scourge.

In those days even the coal was welcomed,
For the peat harvest was often shorthanded
By some war or another.

---

1.   Saint Brigid is the patron saint of blacksmithing, farming, sailors and
     other trades-craft, also poets, printers. She is venerated in the Anglican,
     Catholic, and Eastern Orthodox Churches. Typically connected with
     Celtic cultures.

True Companions

The rolling uplands are alive with late Autumn activity. This year's hunting mentor and I sit on a simple hand-built platform of plywood and 2x4's, the forest's canopy just above us. The fattening squirrels play among the crunchy carpet of mixed hardwood. Even at 2:00 PM, some of the oval shaped oak leaves still hang on, golden fluttering in the intense low-angle rays. The solstice's darkness rapidly approaching.

Here in the very epicenter of nature, we are clad in the most unnatural of colors. No one wears the russet red of hunter's plaid anymore, the so-called American tartan. Traditions change. Too many of the unmentored and under-parented are trying to initiate themselves out here. My generation's round of the "get back to nature movement", recycled, mostly unchanged, marketed and packaged with better graphics. As if liberation simply required shopping at LL Bean, North Face, or REI, then picking up grandpa's rifle and walking to the nearest woodlands. So hi-vis construction worker orange became the standard modern uniform for the rest of us.

I allow two fawns—innocent, their instincts to danger un-honed—to freely pass us within twenty yards. The true hunter never harvests what they will not use. In the silence between woodpeckers tapping out to each other their Morse code of where the dormant bugs are, I think of those without loyal companions, without guides.

The Pileated Woodpeckers' preferred treat, Ash borers,[1] left a few years back, after they chewed through our once-staple hardwood. Some would say humans are like a prion, not really alive, trying to control the brain intelligence of the planet, infecting the natural working order. Like the Chronic Wasting Disease[2] that has infected and tortured so many White Tails in the upper US and Canada. A diseased that arrived after the harvesting of deer slowed, stopped in some places, upsetting the balance that was established for thousands of years by some of my sister-in-law's Cherokee ancestors. Mother Nature's corrective balance is usually *much* uglier than our fashionable vegan and supermarket sensibilities wish to accept.

This weekend's harvest will bless many meals and many bellies, as it did our ancestors, especially true at the Christmas table, a celebration itself of new life, and community renewal. A necessary, and ancient, ritual of victory over darkness, whether pagan, Muslim, Christian or Jew. After the fawns leave our sight, we hear something unseen breaking brush. My sister-in-law leans in, whispering, *Remember, if the offering crosses your path, make a clean kill, do not let it suffer. There is already enough suffering in the world.* The far-off noise fades. The afternoon light fades, the short sun sinks south. We don't see or hear another deer that day.

Meanwhile, the love-mad squirrels are chasing the last unpaired among them around in frantic circles, up and down trees, through brush and bramble, shaking their tails at each other, chattering incessantly. Like bachelors and bachelorettes going into the Winter holidays. No one really wants to be single, with none other to introduce to friends and family, the only one, perpetually, with no engagement announcement, or date secured for New Year's Eve. But like the squirrels, many among them have spent too much time preoccupied with the size of their nuts and shape of their tails to secure a truly loyal companion.

1. Emerald Ash Borer (*Agrilus planipennis*) was first discovered in the American Midwest around Detroit, believed to have arrived in wood pallets from China. Another example of how the offshoring of jobs and sourcing of cheap consumer goods and foreign industrial parts continues to have unplanned consequences and harm America's land, workers, families and natural resources.
2. Due to the generally uncontrollable spread and cross infection of the CWD prion (which eats the brain and cannot be killed like viruses or bacteria) through deer and other wildlife populations, it is generally recommended that hunting harvests of game animals temporarily increase and *all* culled animals be tested for CWD before any human consumption or taxidermy. CWD and similar prion diseases are sometimes referred to as "zombie diseases" as prions are, by their nature, *not* "alive".

Shabbat Dinner, Approaching Hanukkah

"They broke bread in their homes and ate together with glad and sincere hearts."
~Acts 2:46 (NIV)

In another desert, far from the Holy Land, Friday sunset approaches.
The woman of the house lights the candles,

Twin flames in these dark times.

She covers her face,
Not in shame, but reverence.
We are not meant to see G-D,

Only experience the Divine presence.

With the warmth of the candles carried on her smile
My adopted Hebrew mumma greets me, *Shabbat Shalom!...*[1]

I sit around the table with a dozen Israeli Orthodox Jews,
A mélange of Ashkenazi and Sephardi.
Me, the token Polish-American.

To my Catholic Latin ears, the Hebrew is enigmatic,
But somehow my heart understands the prayers—
Blessings over candles, family, wine, bread,

B'ahavah uv'ratzon hin'chal'tanu...[2]

I silently echo my prayer,
Bless us O'Lord in these thy gifts which we are about to receive,
In thy bounty through Christ Our Lord. Amen.[3]

Taking the *Sidur*,[4]
The man of the house, and only American-born Jew,
Suddenly breaks into English on my behalf,
Reading a *Kiddush*[5] passage, *Eshet Chayil.*[6]

During this patriarchal religious ritual
I hear women sincerely honored more than at any feminist gathering
      I've ever attended
In communities or eight years of ivory tower academia.

Before dinner, a broad and tall middle-aged man with piercing eyes
Has been exhibiting his fondness for photography and politics.

This ex-military man, clearly skilled in all forms of sharpshooting,
Begins *Netilat Yadayim*.[7]

Barukh atah Adonai
Eloheinu, melekh ha'olam
Hamotzi lechem min ha'aretz. Amein[9]

Though I only observe the ritual,
Somehow, I feel the sins of my family slowly washing away from my
    heart.
I silently echo my prayer,
As we forgive those who trespass against us...[8]

At table's center, *Challah*, braiding people to the land,
Jews and Christians.

The respect given this food reminds me of my Polish and Slavic
    traditions,
The sacredness of the grain harvest.
Chelb for everyday guests, special *oplatek* on *Wigilia*.[10]

Silently I pray,
Give us this day our daily bread...[11]

Together we all intone, *Amen.*

Mumma smiles,
"*Yalla, yalla!* Let's eat!"

1. *Shabbat Shalom* (Hebrew: "Sabbath of Peace"), traditional Jewish Sabbath greeting.
2. *B'ahavah uv'ratzon hin'chal'tanu* (Hebrew: "You have lovingly and willingly given us for an inheritance...").
3. A pre-Communion (the Host) ritual prayer.
4. *Sidur* (Hebrew) the *Shabbat* (Jewish Sabbath) prayer book.
5. *Kiddush*: a ceremonial prayer over the Shabbat dinner food.
6. *Eshet Chayil* (Hebrew: "woman of valor") a traditional Jewish from Proverbs 10:10-31 (NJB).
7. *Netilat Yadayim* (Hebrew: "hand washing") a ritual done before breaking the *Shabbat* bread.
8. The Lord's Prayer (a universal Christian prayer).
9. Hebrew: "Blessed are you, Lord", "Our G-d, sovereign of the universe", "Who brings forth from the earth. Amen."
10. *Chelb* (Polish: a standard table bread). *Oplatek* (Polish: unleavened bread (like a Catholic Communion wafer, shared with Christmas Eve guests and

paired with mutual blessings). *Wigilia*, the Polish Christmas Eve celebration. Similar to Jewish *matzo* bread.

11. The "Our Father" (a universal Christian prayer).

First Snow
(2022)

"The Christmas tree is one of those customs which are food for the sold, nourishment for the inner man. And the more primordial the material they use, the more promising these customs are for the future." - Carl G. Jung[1]

Winter's chill arrives suddenly this year. The Indian Summer stretching all the way to early November. The leaves falling before the thermometer, then abruptly plunging 35°F in one day. Now for weeks, a bone numbing dreary rain, just above icy, and gloomy firmament seems to cling to everyone and everything. Today, I venture out into the first snow, grateful for my green wool greatcoat and Scottish-granite-flecked tweed-herringbone-gloves. I move among the cheerless in my community grocery, pharmacy, toy store and my own psychotherapy clinic, wondering if Yule Logs, twinkle lights, or Hanukkah candles can still defrost the ice in their hearts. Can we still be ushered into a new era, or is this the time when our history freezes over in a post-modern malaise?

1.   Gerster, Georg (1957). "C.G. Jung Speaking: Interviews and Encounters". *Die Weltwoche*. Zurich, Switzerland. (p 353-358).

Winter's Cloak

Have you ever noticed how after a soft snowfall,
Or an unrelenting blizzard,
When the sense of time ceases,
Everything becoming fractal vision.
When winter's bare sharpness becomes pleasantly round, soft and smooth,

She gestures,

Our attention toward the incubation.

The cloudless February sky
Warming moving wetting us.

Everything is stirring, but not yet waking.

With Her winter cloak of cerulean blue above,
We convene in sun-bathed woolen-wrapped silence,
Nestled among the folds of her vestments

No longer purely white

For She has been traveling with us through frigid wilderness,

Pilgrims in our own country.

Wandering Candles

"The Light shines in the darkness, and the darkness has not overcome it." (John 1:4-9 - NJB)

December 13th, St. Lucy's Feast Day.[1]
Tonight, across the American upper Midwest, and the Canadian
        Prairie,
No matter secular or religious, families are celebrating the "Saint of
        Light"
Honored traditions, brought from Sweden.

Ginger biscuits and houses, saffron buns, sweet bread, filling home
        ovens, and Meijers, Kroger, Jewel, IGA, Safeway, Festival
        grocer bakeries.
Mulled wine, usually joyfully acquired from 3rd Coast Midwest
        vineyard stock
                (criminally underappreciated by the Napa and
                New England snobs)
Sometimes humbly brewed in barn, basement, or tool shed.

A local, unassuming but bright girl with a still-undiscovered voice,
Trained mostly on Top 40 Country, or youngest boy cousin, oft
        forgotten at large gatherings,
Both still listen for reindeer bells in the dark woods,

Sends out a warm stream of *Sancta Lucia*[2] through the still night,

Enticing the dark solstice sullen
And slow-dropping snowflakes,
To dance in the half-moon pale numina.

The girl, voted by classmates "most likely to bring out the best in
        others,"
Dresses in white,
Then wraps and ties the winterberry-red ribbon or sash.

She hears her Mother's reminder to walk into the less trodden paths
        with love,
But not naively succumb to others fatal flaws.
Before stepping out into the night, she lights the candles, adorns the
        crown.

1. Saint Lucia (Lucy) of Syracuse, Italy. Widely adopted and celebrated by both pagan, Christian and even atheist Scandinavians.
2. Translated by Teodoro Cottrau (19th Century), the first Neapolitan language song to be translated into modern Italian. Modern versions of this ancient hymn made popular by Elvis Presley (*Elvis for Everyone!*, 1965) and Bing Crosy (*101 Gang Songs,* 1961).

A weak pacifism, moral cowardice.

Yule Log
"Love is not an affectionate feeling, but a steady wish for the loved person's ultimate good as far as it can be obtained." - C.S. Lewis

If the Creator gives us nothing more than we can endure, the devil gives us the filthy residue. So scrape it into the Solstice fire kindled from a properly prepared Yule Log. After the blaze of your grief cools, mix the ash with that extra stress fat you've been carrying around your guts, by fasting a bit, from that indulgent type of "agony". Mix a new lather, then cleanse your heart, and later your hands, of yesteryears' messes.

The Covid Carnivals
(Winter Solstice 2020)

In Jesus's time there were several celestial bodies announcing the
    change,
Ushering in the witnesses to a birth in Pisces's cosmic tidepool,
    and the funeral pyre
Of the old era. This Winter Solstice, only two stars are conjunct:
Saturn and Jupiter, *Senex* and *Puer.*
Old grouchy Saturn, with his slightly neurotic ISTJ nostalgia.[1]
Young whining Jupiter, with his naïve ahistorical loincloth.
Both unemployed, terrified, and on the brink of being homeless on
    the streets of L.A.

What no one is talking about? The Holy Spirit has been given
Its severance pay, a cheap gold-plated watch, a doughy taco party in
    the conference room...
And-then was banished, utterly.
In its absence (filling the void, forming out of thin air):
An unmonitored kindergarten
Of tantruming fundamentalisms and pouting dualities,
Hurling napalm Legos at each other.
No matter who "wins", America loses.

1.   Meyers-Briggs Personality Test (MBTI). The ISTJ type's negative traits
    include pathological nostalgia, stubborn refusal to innovate, curmudgeon
    behavior and thinking.

Eternal Light

Everyone's tongue is on fire,
With few good words
To script into Christmas or Hanukkah greetings.
Chag urim sameach or peace be with you[1] –
Are absent from the formulaic tables.
Who can recall the letters on dreidels or
Why we both decorate with lights?[2]
We are a house divided, and prayer has become a political act.

1. *Hag rim sameach* (Hebrew: "happy holiday/festival of light"), a traditional
    Hanukkah greeting and blessing. "Peace be with you", a traditional
    Christian and Jewish greeting, also used in the (Hebrew: "*Shalom
    Aleichem*").
2. 2 Maccabees 10:6-8 (found in the Apocryphal Gospels) refers to the origins
    of Hanukkah, related to the Greek's cultural and martial war against the
    Jews. Also the importance of communal celebration. 1 Peter 2:9. John 1:5,
    "And the light shines in the darkness, and darkness could not overpower
    it."

Journey to Graceland
(2024)

"In the end the Shadow was only a small and passing thing: there was light and high beauty for ever beyond its reach." – J.R.R. Tolkien[1]

By now in NYC, there's snow on the ground...[2]

Some homes have the eerie silence of emotional nuclear winter.
For now, we each must endure arduous distances between our hearts.
That old melody again echoes in your waking moments,

Merry Christmas from Dixie, to everyone tonight...

You arrive where there was once sanctuary,
Believing there will be a natural hospitality, normal human
     kindness, instead,
There's no room at the inn, crowed at you, three times.

Set back on the road, like you are un-kosher, *haram*, or a demonic
     creature,
Your light, twisted into their gaslight.
Your peace offering vulgar to their half-closed ears
Filled with the both straw and opium,[3]
Both sold at the Circus Maximus's endless rallies.
You see their raised fists clenched around what you suspect is their
     silver pieces.

You now understand, you have become the scapegoat,
Who later they will try to slaughter,
To absolve their own mistakes and hubris.

Perhaps if we each could just see the *Graceland all alit,*

Our hearts would be called back to the spirit of King's brotherhood.
Christmas-time is not meant to be a Cold War.
The Light can be an ambassador, illuminating both high roads and
     low roads.

From all across the nation, it's peaceful Christmas time...

1. *Lord of the Rings: The Return of the King.*
2. Some italicized lyrics referenced are from *Christmas in Dixie* by the famous American rock and roll group, Alabama.
3. C.G. Jung on the "Religious Function of the Psyche". Jung's message is an expansion on the Biblical principle of "giving to Caesar what is Caesar's, and to G-d what is G-D's". When people mix religion with State and State with religious needs, great confusion and hubris results. For these reasons, the American Constitution, among others, separates Church and State, and ensures freedom of religion and creed (or profession to none).

What happens to a person who only sees negative space in a place of exuberant pageantry?

Galilean Epiphany

"Jesus said, 'Mary!' She turned round then and said to him in Hebrew, 'Rabbuni!'" (John 20:16, NJB)[1]

Who was the Magdalene when Christ was born?
Was she the daughter of a man who reeked of the fish he gutted
    each morning?
Could we find her swaying her hips on a brothel floor?
Was she sprawled over the lap of some low-level Roman bureaucrat?
The heiress to a sleazy Galilean tax collector?
Or just a street waif selling dried pomegranate seeds and trinkets,
    surviving on a few shekels?

Or an urbane Jew of Hellenist grooming and Roman resources?
Was her mother a fallen Essene prophet?[2]
Was she already proclaiming love would be at the center of all
    things?[3]
Or was she Anna's niece, playing with a simple doll on the Temple
    steps,
While Mary presented Jesus?

And no more stoning circles.

1. Rabbuni (Hebrew: Teacher, or Master in the mentoring relationship).
2. The Dead Sea Scrolls are believed to be writings of the Essene Jewish sect of the 1st Century C.E./A.D. The Essenes mystical Jewish sect residing by the Sea of Galilee. They are mentioned by the Roman author Philo of Alexandria—"Every Good Man is Free XI-XII"), and "Hypothetica or Apology for the Jews 11.1-19. The Jewish historian, Josephus, described parallels between the Essene Jews and the Greek Pythagoreans— "Antiquities of the Jews 18.1.2&5 (11, 18-22), and "The Jewish War" (2.8.1-14, pg. 117-166).
3. Story of Jesus and the Samaritan woman at the well (John 4: 1-42).

Tinsel Town

Ornaments, adornments of what we adore. The Christmas Tree, *axis mundi*[1], the holiday home altar. Flint, Michigan, 1992.

I remember grandmother's tree. Some years, fresh cut near Frankenmuth. The village's Alpine-styled German architecture, old wooden bridges, Oktoberfest, like a moment in Innocent Art. And the still-impressive Bronner's, a Christmas goods store open 362 days a year, like the windowless color maze of an Ikea store. By comparison, Chicago's Kris Kringle Market is charming but still small potatoes. Other years, the *Tannenbaum* was selected at the cracked asphalt lot of a Frank's Nursery and Crafts, trucked down from da' U.P., perhaps Marquette or Christmas, Michigan.

Christmas Eve, with true Polish and Prussianized[2] tradition, America's burden and genius, a roomful of baffling buzz, our whole family lights and adorns the tree. Though the candles are no longer wax and wick, the large electric lights, blown glass globes, Polish crystal and chromed birds hearken back to an age of innocence,[3] when angels sang across the Rust Belt (the immigrant's promised land). The tree's glow recalled the fabled arches that used to illume downtown Flint, one of the first American cities to usher in the new era's light. When Gary, Cleveland, Flint, Toledo and Milwaukee were each their own tinsel town, at least to first-generation kids.

Every Christmas, the tree, each family's centerpiece art installation, altar and *axis mundi*.

1. The *axis mundi*, Latin for "world axis," is an idea found in various world religions. It is a vector that that connects the heavens, the earth, and the underworld. This axis is often seen as a central point around which the world revolves and serves as a link between different planes of existence. In many cultures, the *axis mundi* is symbolized by various objects or places. Naturally, the religions that describe an *axis mundi* place great stock in it.

2. After the Fall of Poland (Partitions of the 1700s), The Prussian, Russian and Austro-Hungarian Empires collectively conspired to carve up historical Poland and force assimilate Poland's lands and people into their domains. During the Great Migrations to America (1880-1924), over 25 million immigrants arrived. Polish people, hailing from Polish cities and villages, speaking Polish, living Polish customs, were often marked at Ellis Island (including other American ports of reception, and European departure) as "German" due to their government papers (issued by

Prussia), and others from their port of departure, often Poland's Gdansk (German: "Danzig"). Those officially marked Poles were counted around 2.5 million or 10 percent from the Great Migration period. According to David Siwik's studies on Polish populations in Michigan and surrounding American Midwest highlights the problems of American census records not matching passenger manifests. The U.S. Census enumerated people by birthplace, not ethnicity, often mixing Austrians, Russians, Germans/Prussians (the three Partitioning Powers). Siwik's work attempts to correct these historical documentation errors by identifying the true numbers of the Polish immigrant population by their mother tongue (native/first language) on U.S. Census documents. A resulting sample is telling—three-quarters of the Calumet (Illinois) Poles (often labeled as "German") studied emigrated from German/Prussian Partition territory of historical Poland. See https://ethnicity.lib.mtu.edu/groups_Poles_print.html .

3. Edith Wharton's novel, *Age of Innocence,* winner of the 1921 Pulitzer Prize.

Polish Rhapsody: After The 12 Days of Christmas
(for Norman Davies)
*All species highlighted are native or domesticated to Poland.

Twelve Days of Polish Christmas gifted me...

Beholding an osprey alighting the *Cielętniki* Linden tree.[1]

Glimpsing two White Eagles spiraling,
Mieszko and Jan Paweł II, delightfully.[2]

Seeing waddling three Blue Swedish Ducks,
Faith for the blues, sending hope skyward, and Torch Lake-blue
clarity.

Hearing four Calandra Larks singing,
Like an Orthodox Priest chanting, *In the Dark Night,*[3] sweetly.

Marveling five amber rings glowing
Since the Partitions,
Left in the *Sejm,* by Pulaski and Rejtan, Kościuszko and Joselewicz,
and Prince Poniatowski.[4]

Sighting six Egyptian Geese migrating [5]
From decades of cold alienation,
Back to ancestral homes, gratefully.

Considering seven Mute Swans, silently awaiting
The Holy Spirit's brisk December visitation, pensively.

Appreciating eight Kaszubi 6 maidens hosting their Beloved
Community.

Regarding Nine Zakopane [7] ladies generously delightedly dancing
Through the market, manor house, and beggars' alley.

Witnessing ten *Szlachta*[8] persevering,
Guarding the heart of Europe,
The crossroads of history.

Feeling eleven *Płock* [9] fiddlers bowing ballads,
Faithful to our true wealth, culturally.

Perceiving twelve hurdy-gurdy's calling us

To *Jasna Gora,* [10]
Resolutely.

1. The largest tree in Poland, estimated to be at least 550 years old. A common lime, or Linden tree, sacred to Poles since pagan times.
2. Mieszko the 1st was the first ruler of the independent Polish state (960-992). Jan Paweł II (Karol Józef Wojtyła) the first Polish Catholic Pope was a major leader of the *Solidarność* Solidarity Movement which ultimately liberated Poland from Soviet Communism.
3. A mystical Catholic and Orthodox Christian Christmas about the birth of Christ, popular in Poland and Ukraine.
4. *Sejm* (Polish Parliament). *Rejtan: The Fall of Poland* (Polish: *Upadek Polski*) by Jan Matejko. Berek (Dov Baer) Joselewicz (Hebrew: ברק דב בר יוסלביץ) a Polish-Jewish leader of the all-Jewish Calvary during the Kosciuszko Uprising 1794. Prince Józef Antoni Poniatowski of Poland. Kaszubi (Polish: *Kashubian*).
5. Egyptian Geese*(Alopochen Aegyptiacus)*, native to sub-Saharan Africa, were introduced to mainland Europe after being imported to the UK at ornamental birds. In modern times they are considered invasive.
6. *Kaszubi* (Kashubians) are known for their hospitality and elaborate and colorful floral needlework reflecting Poland's richly diverse agricultural and natural landscape.
7. Zakopane is a resort/destination mountainous region in south Poland, known for its conservative Highlander (*Goral*) culture, unique architecture, high art woodworking, and other traditional folk craft.
8. The middle and upper classes of pre-Partition (late 1700s) Poland, estimated 20+% of the population (compared to their Western European counterparts numbering less than 1% of their respective populations). Historically, the *Szlachta* served in the leadership/political class, earning their titles and land primarily by service in the Polish army/knights.
9. See Maria Pomianowska, the premiere "Suka" (*Płock* fiddle, a Polish instrument similar to violin) musician, who has performed the resurrected instrument extensively, both solo and with Yo-Yo Ma's Silk Road Orchestra, and other fusion ensembles.
10. The monastery of the Polish Black Madonna (Lady of Czestochowa), the Queen of Poland.

Seven Flowers of the Midwest Winter

There's the simple English Ivy we braid for our homes' mantles and hearths.
I think of all the arranged marriages, like Mary and Joseph,
Unlikely bonds formed through deliberate slow patience and spiritual discernment.
Enduring through life's emotional cold snaps and hot temper love droughts.

Then, the Christmas Cactus's bountiful fuchsia floral waterfall.
Like a mariachi band unabashedly wailing *Feliz Navidad*, on repeat, from a turquoise 4x4 truck,
Cruising from home, Chicago's Pilsen neighborhood, to their cousins' Aurora and Elgin office parties.[1]

Oh those persnickety poinsettias, the bane of greenhouse workers north of Dixie!
Like newborn babes, everything and anything can accidentally injure them.
So if you can keep its flowers blooming past New Year's Eve, consider it fate,
An encouraging omen for the coming year's success.

Also, mistletoe mischief, not just the debauched custom of skirt chasing and trouser teasing.
Vitality and boldness are needed to embrace love's transitory opportunities at life's thresholds.
Known to people taken and sent from the Isles into diaspora, to work and slave in foreign lands,
Perhaps never to see their true love again.

Christmas Rose,
Purging psyche's parasites, the squirming embedding tendrils dropped by Medusa.
Enduring, reblooming, the more its thorniness has been pruned,
Full and delicate love rediscovered in life's later half.

Michigan Holly,
Known for ages to the Huron and Wyandot Nations to cure cabin fever.[2]
Winter's bleakness brightens, when our kitchen windows frame those crimson clusters

Against the polar vortex crusted canvas of mid-January.

Our commonplace office palm with another fortuitous name, Dragon
Blood Tree.[3]
For the first time in 33 years, just prior to Advent, I'm delighted to
witness its bloom,
Announced with nearly overpowering fragrance, and spring-clear
lingering sap tears.

Soon, we suspect the Mystical Rose will squeeze a bit of that Edenic
sweetness back out the
    dragon's head. [4]

1.   Aurora and Elgin, Illinois, both suburbs of Chicago, have the highest
Hispanic and Latino populations in the American Midwest, and account
for nearly half the population of two cities.
2.   *Ilex verticillate,* aka. fever bush (Native American/First Nations),
Winterberry, American holly. Drugs as psychological aids. "Decoction of
winterberry bark taken as an emetic for craziness." Native American
Ethnobotany Database. Herrick, James William, 1977, Iroquois Medical
Botany, State University of New York, Albany, PhD Thesis, page 373.
http://naeb.brit.org/uses/17727/
3.   *Dracaena fragrans,* (aka. Dragon Blood Tree, Corn Palm, Happy Plant) a
common office plant.
4.   Reference to Mary in Revelations and (Genesis 3:15 – DRB) (Revelations
12:1-17 – NJB).

The First Supper
(December 24, 2021)
"He will be your joy and delight and many will rejoice at his birth." (Luke 1:14)

On the eve of our cosmic cycle
Twelve guests have arrived for the first supper.

I proudly plate my twelve-ish dishes,
Honoring the Apostles and company.

For *Matka Boża*,[1]
Makowiec.
Abundant beautiful fertility, wrapped in the bread of life.

For Mary Magdalene, Apostle to the Apostles,
Oliwki.[2]
Anointing our tongues with fraternal love.

For Peter,
Kandyzowany imbir.[3]
Helping us to digest every difficult bit of the Word, with a spoonful
of sweetness.

For Andrew,
Kielbasa.[4]
Reminding us the gentle babe, and his parents, are not impotent.

For Mark,
Kompot.[5]
Like at Cana, reminding us patience makes the heart fonder, and joy
sincere.

For Philip,
Chałka.[6]
To break bread with our neighbors, in the spirit of Shabbat.

For John,
Kluski.[7]
Cautioning us to beware hospitality from the poison-hearted and
whiners.

For Bartholomew (Nathanial)
Daktyle i figi.[8]

Once wasting away days under a defoliated tree, now called to abundant and purposeful living.

For Jude,
Barszcz z uszkami.[9]
Like little boats, floating us through seemingly hopeless, murky waters.

For James,
Marynowany śledź i szprot.[10]
Once vinegar shame, now fishers of men.

For Thomas,
Bigos.[11]
Some have to stew life's great mysteries all afternoon.

For James the Younger,
Babka.[12]
Watch silently for first proving, add fruit of the vine, entomb in the stone oven, let rise, add spirit.

For Simon Peter,
Ogórki.[13]
Without faith, a perpetually salty inclination eventually pickles us.

For Matthew
Chruściki,[14]
Lifting us in sweet bliss.

For Judas Iscariot,
Krupnik.[15]
Sweetness on the lips tonight, hangover tomorrow.

For Matthias,
Now sitting-in for Judas,
Who tried to eat money instead of bread, the plate is empty.[16]

---

1. *Matka Boża* (Polish: Mother of God). *Makowiec* (poppy seed bread).
2. *Oliwki* (olives).
3. *Kandyzowany imbir* (candied ginger).
4. *Kiełbasa* (Polish Sausage).
5. *Kompot* (fruit juice, usually apple/berry based).
6. *Chałka* (braided bread, similar to Jewish Challa served on Shabbat).
7. *Kluski* (noodles with dried fruit, nuts, poppy seeds).

8. *Daktyle i figi* (dates and figs).
9. *Barszcz z uszkami* (mushroom dumplings in red boarsch).
10. *Marynowany śledź i szprot* (marinated dill herring with pickled onions).
11. *Bigos* (cabbage-based stew with carrots, caramelized onions, prunes, tomato sauce, mushrooms, sweet vinegar and savory spices.
12. *Babka* (iced dessert cake w dried fruit, baked in a Bundt pan).
13. *Ogórki* (Polish-style dill pickles).
14. *Chruściki* ("angel wings", a sweet pastry similar to *kolachky*).
15. *Krupnik* ("fire vodka", honey vodka blended with heavy mulling spices).
16. After Judas Iscariot betrayed Jesus and killed himself, the remaining core eleven Apostles voted the Apostle Matthias to join their council and replace Judas. At Polish Christmas Eve traditional rituals, an empty place setting is left for an unexpected neighbor or pilgrim.

Lanterns in the Dark Wood
(Michigan)

My girlfriend and I are northbound in a driving blizzard,
Headed for a weekend get-away with family.
I steer my low-slung Chevy Monte Carlo through the dark.

Following the other cars through shadowy forest tunnels,
I'm astounded at the trust we place in snowplow crews.
We follow them through sepulchral forest tunnels.

At high speed, it's easy to slip into a trance.
Flakes thick as Vesuvian volcanic ash
Spin into a vortex—somewhere just beneath our wheels.

Visibility is mere inches past the cars' hoods. GPS is equally
Useless. No driver can see safe path from unforgiving ditch.
It seems Heaven's light cannot reach us here.

For nearly two-hundred miles, the reflective stanchions and green
markers
(Crusted in ice) hide all signs of exit from the dark wood.
I'm mindful of the precipice, mere feet from the passenger's tires.

Only the plowman's truck we trust, with its Fresnel-lensed lights like
fireplace hearths,
Or pilgrims' lanterns at a medieval city gate glowing in the spectra of
safety
Orient us to the path.

Dark Nights of the Soul

In the darkest days, prepare the temple.

Confess. What clout has wounded innocence?
Unobtrusive reflection, not encounter groups.

The necessity, to be reborn in the Heart of Humanity,
Arrives during humbling conditions.[1]

When institutionalized, profanity demands a journey
To birth a new self.

After the darkest night of the soul,
Generosity.

Birth, Crucifixion, Resurrection,
Beginnings without end.[2]

Make table for two or twenty,[3]
Center the wreath, the eternal cycle of greening.

No matter Winter's vast bleakness
Under the cold mantle, faithful ever-greening.

Tend the alter within,
Sweet light, carry us through the darkest nights.

Purple,
Pain and repentance.

Red,
How have we bled for common oaths?

Pink,
The flush of our rejoicing faces, ashen so long.

White,
Cleanse us, embark a new cycle.

Theotokos, implore us to labor, a bit longer,[4]

Until the darkness subsides.

Theotokos, help us hold this tautness,

In the liminal spaces.

When all we wish to do is forget, help us remember what wounded innocence.

1. The concept of the "dark night of the soul" originated from the Trappist monk, Saint John of the Cross, and his poetry, which examines the effects of depression on spirit and soul. See further reading from a Jungian Psychology perspective in *Dark Night of the Soul: a Guide for Finding Your Way Through Life's Ordeals* by Thomas Moore.
2. In Jungian Analyst, Sam Keen's book, *Beginnings Without End* (1977), written amidst the American 1960s-1970s Cultural Revolutions, Keen introduces his personal testimony about his inner and outer life being upended (much due to his own choices). The book is philosophy, an instruction manual and *cautionary tale*, about what happens under the conditions of a society increasingly influenced and guided by Post-Modern principles, or when one adopts Post-Modernist philosophies as their dominant cosmology/personal mythology/ or totalitarian worldview. Keen intimately shares and instructs what occurs when the "old gods/God", old authorities, old paradigms are *suddenly*, quickly, radically, removed from contact with the human self. Keen's book examines his personal psychological journey in which he comes to terms with the very difficult consequences of not only the generational American Cultural Revolution, but also his subsequent, extended and personal (but relatable) Dark Night of the Soul.
3. (Matthew 18:20 – NJV) "For where two or three meet in my name, I am there among them."
4. *Theotokos* is the Eastern Orthodox (especially used in Greek and Russian churches) name for the Mother of God, especially the Black Madonnas.
5. For further resources on depression resulting from catastrophic change, see also the Buddhist, Pema Chodron's, *When Things Fall Apart: Heart Advice for Difficult Times* (2000).

Santa Klaus

Whether they were raised with religion or not,
No matter the strength of their faith or nihilism,
At some point in their life, a great-many children address to Saint
Nicholas,
For their hopes, preventative wishes, and prayers.

Often, after the adults have astonishingly failed
To provide them with even glimpses of hopeful future.
And when that fails, there is only the survival
Of quick pleasures, cheap entertainment, unapologetic hedonism.

So let your kids believe in Santa Clause or Father Christmas, to
respect Saint Nicholas, and try-out their faith in the transpersonal.
Because they may not believe in *anything* else (including you).
Their fragile faith and may already have severed from
10,000 cruel cuts.[1]

Who is Santa Clause, really?
An adult who believes in children and
Their capacity for potent goodness.
The spirit of Saint Nicholas is a benevolent adult, mentor, caretaker,
elder, a sage.
If you take that away,
They may even stop believing in the idea of messiah's and teachers
all together.

What kind of world will we have,
Without imagination, whimsey, magic, or the transcendent,
What will humanity be left with
When the children grow up as
A jaded generation teaching another terrified generation teaching
another adrift generation[2]
Not to have faith in *anything*?

---

1. Rule of "10,000 hours" to learn a skill, solidly. Social learning follows
    similar realities, in that, 10,000 negatively reinforcements will also teach.
    But it will teach, especially children, only to expect the cruelty of the
    world, never it's justice.

2. In studies of intergenerational trauma, the lifestyle habits, mental attitudes, and especially worldview, are passed down/taught directly from generation to generation. This is accomplished via active parenting and indirectly via meta-patterns, unconscious habits, "I don't know why I do that___" social modeling. This is understood colloquially as the "loss of wisdom" from a people/community, or ignorance of how to live in rhythm with life. More seriously, this can me an almost total loss of basic life skills, how to create stability, or even practical survival skills (executive functioning, task management). This is *not* accounted for by a neurological defect (ie. brain damage, lead/heavy metal poisoning, invitro drug exposure, fetal alcohol syndrome, or other teratogens) or malformation of the brain's "software" (i.e. genetic inheritance of low IQ, Down Syndrome, etc.).

In the Dark Night
(in memory of William Butler Yeats)

In the darkest nights of the darkest years
We discover most how much the world needs Christmas,
How much *we* need Christmas.

When Midnight Mass and wassailing around the apple trees
Has been bartered for Black Friday and New Year's orgies,[1]
Where heritage lies, dismembered and bleeding, on the altar of
Dionysius,
As with Yeats' ceremony of innocence, drowning in an anarchistic
tsunami we have ourselves
        unleashed.[2]

The monks in Ukraine understand the dark night more than anyone
this year.[3]

In the darkest nights of the darkest years
We fathom how much we need the Divine Heart.

1. *In the Dark Night* (aka. *Sleep Jesus*), a traditional Ukrainian Christmas
   Carol/Chant. See performance by Monks of Svetogorskaya Lavra, Ukraine.
2. *"This fifty days of preparation is called in their barbarian speech the Exmas rush....But
   the festival comes, then most ofothe citizens, being exhausted with the Rush, lie in bed till
   noon. And on the day after Exmas they are very grave, being internally disordered by the
   supper and the drinking and reckoning how much they have spent on gifts and on the
   wine..."* C.S. Lewis, "Xmas and Christmas: A Lost Chapter from
   Herodotus".
3. W.B. Yeats, *The Second Coming.*

Unorthodox Christmas

"Be impatient with easy explanations
and teach that part of the mind that wants to
know everything
not to begin questions
it cannot answer."

- Tobar Phadraic, trans. by David Whyte

Unorthodox Christmas
(a letter to Walt Whitman - January 2022)[1]

I watch my nieces play under the boughs of a Christmas tree.
Each has one eye and hand on their new toys,
The other on the clan's new baby, my godson.

It's his first Christmas.
Born in a time of ever-encroaching darkness—
    Plague,
    Apathetic and pestilential,
    The Republic on the verge of verge of schism[2]?

Our Midwest Scotts-Irish clan has gathered,
Among the rolling dells of southern Wisconsin.
Our hosts, a fisherman and his wife (both retired Methodist pastors).
Me, the token Catholic.
But this year we're all orthodox, celebrating Christmas in January.

These times seem apocalyptic—
    Institutions eroding,
    Everyone quitting,
    Everything being canceled
        (except autocratic thinking).
    As each decade passes, we seem to lose more and more of our
humanity
        (our souls and *fratria*).
    I wonder if soon there will be no place for God,
        (let alone the human condition).

I think of Whitman—
"There will soon be no more priests.... The gangs of kosmos and
prophets *en masse* shall take their place. A new order shall rise and
they shall be the priests of man, and every man shall be his own
priest."[1]

Oh Walt, how naïve you were,
How brashly you encouraged the next seven generations
To abandon the concept of Seven Generations.[2]

Walt, you idiot
Didn't you realize

——

Gangs and prophets *en masse* always take what's most shiny
And leave the rest to rot
In the overgrown grasses of unkept traditions
And gutters of history?[3]

Walt, you fool,
You never imagined,
Someday, they'll use even your poetry
As toilet paper.

1. Walt Whitman, *Leaves of Grass* (1855).
2. The Native American/First Nations concept of Seven Generations.
3. W.B. Yeates, "the center cannot hold".

Invisible Hands

"The communication of the dead is tongued with fire beyond the language of the living." – T.S. Eliot, *4 Quartets*

Christ-Mass, four priests lead an overflowing church in the Our Father Prayer.

We know the Divine by many titles,

Quakingly whispered, steadily chanted, joyfully sung.
> *Hallowed be thy Divine name...*

An ancestral crowd reaches out to us through the suddenly thin veil.
> *On Earth as it is in Heaven...*

What summons us to check our ego at the portal of Mystery?
> *Thy will be done...*

Each of us alone before the Divine—
> *Forgive us our trespasses...*

Still, we gather here together, hand-in-hand with the Other.
> *As we forgive those who trespass against us...*

Invisible hands aid us with an assuringly firm squeeze,
> *Do not let us fall into temptation...*

And walk beside us as we brave the coming nights without tonight's light.
> *But deliver us from evil...*

Auto-Excommunicatus

"Be impatient with easy explanations and teach that part of the mind that wants to know everything not to begin questions it cannot answer." - Tobar Phadraic[2], trans. by David Whyte

I remember when my father stopped attending church,
It was Christmas.

What happens to a man who can no longer hear Christmas's joy,
When nothing in his soul stirs in the presence of a gifted choir,
When he succumbs to the Solstice's darkness, in an eternal Dark
Night of the Soul?

The beginning of his *auto-excommunicatus.*[2]

[1]. An Irish Saint associated with the well of Saint Patrick.
[2]. To excommunicate oneself, remove from communion, as with especially a Christian church.

Christmas Eve 2023
(Church of the Nativity, Bethlehem)[1]
"Christmas is not modern. Christmas is not Marxian." - G.K. Chesterson

As Erving Goffman noted, when we lose the private identity, all that
remains is the public identity, and that then is burdened with too
much.

Preparing to host a tableful and home full of guests—
    Catholics,
    Protestants,
    Gnostics,
    Pagans,
    the spiritually unaffiliated,
    post-Christians—
I see the news break about the Holy Land.
Christmas, the gathering of fellowship in peace,
Canceled.

A curious act of "solidarity".

As it is said about the true meaning of poem, look to the text, not
what the poet says.
I continue mixing beet salad, hands looking bloodied, and begin
quietly singing.

Oh come all ye faithful, to Bethlehem...
    (to the empty churches)

Oh come oh come Emmanuel, and ransom captive Israel [3, 7, 8]
    (among the gullible and ahistorical does propaganda easily
    travel)

That mourns in lonely exile here...[2, 3]
    (where all the tired hatred tropes appear) [3, 4, 7]

To us the path of knowledge show...
    (which does not from the river to the sea flow) [2, 3, 7, 8]

From the depths of hell your people save...[4]
    (from those who turn the Religion of Peace into a quick path
    to the grave) [3, 4, 7, 8]

Oh come o bright and Morning Star... [5]

92

(speak to us as *Sayyida Siddiquah*) [6]

Dispel the shadows of the night...[7, 8]
  (each nation's apathy and ignorance is our collective plight)

Bid our sad divisions cease. [3, 4, 7, 8]

1. The Church of the Nativity in Bethlehem is built over the geographical spot where Jesus is believed to have been born.
2. Between 2014 and 2020, UN agencies spent $4.5 billion in Gaza ($600 million just in 2020). See also the Ad Hoc Liaison Committee's annual donations coordinated from some Arab nations, EU, USA, Japan. Since 1994, the United States (USAID) has provided $5.2 billion to Palestinians. Total global aid to Palestinians is estimated $40+ billion (1994-2020). Palestinian's two primary ideological and political supporters, provide some funds—Quatar (estimated in 100's of millions), and Iran providing $100+ million annually. In 2005, Hamas won elections in 2006 (after an armed coup) in the Palestinian territories. Hamas controls/administers most of the revenue from taxed imports, the economy and most of the social welfare program distributions.
3. The Hamas charter principle of *dar al harb* (Article 6, 11, 13, 15). Hamas states there is *no negotiated settlement possible* (ie. the internationally proposed "two or three-state solution", or *peace* with Israel/Jews). The charter states *jihad is the only solution* (Article 13). Comparing Israel with "imperialist-colonialist movement" while *exempting* themselves and current/historical Islamic Imperialist practices in conquered (and yet to-be conquered) lands (Arabic: *dar al Islam* or *dar al harb*) is particularly contradictory and hypocritical in Hamas's and others' critiques of the State of Israel, and of historical and present Eastern and Western empires, colonialism, and current multicultural/multi-religious democratic sovereign states.
4. 1988 Hamas Covenant (the organization's founding document) and its revised charter (2017), *A Document of General Principles and Policies*, (Arabic: وثيقة المبادئ والسياسات العامة لحركة حماس). The charter clearly outlines the strong promotion of "lesser Jihad" (Arabic: al-jihād al-aṣghar) which Jihad through *violence*. Globally, modern Islamic groups, scholars and schools rather tend to promote the personal religious and character improvement and purification, the inner or "greater Jihad" (Arabic: al-jihād al-akbar). Greater Jihad has historically been promoted by Sufi Islam (known more commonly as the "Whirling Dervishes" of Egypt, Turkey, Europe, USA, etc.). Hamas is based in the Salafist sect of Islam.
5. "Morning Star" is one of the many honorary titles of the Virgin Mary, The Madonna, *Theotokos*, Mother of Jesus.
6. *Sayyida* (Arabic: "Lady", in the sense of fullness/complete embodiment of archetypal royal womanhood). Siddiquah (Arabic: "she who confirms the truth.") In Islam, the Virgin Mary is exalted in highest regard above all living women, and all women in the Old Testament, Christian Bible and Quran.
7. The Preamble to the 1988 Charter stated, "Israel will exist and will continue to exist *until Islam invalidates it, just at Islam invalidated others* [emphasis

added] before Israel." This is referencing other historical sovereign nations and people and religions that Islam has conquered. Additionally, much of Hamas's purpose and justification for their existence, organization and actions are based on long-debunked anti-Semitic conspiracy theories and xenophobic tropes (Article 20, 22, 28, 35).

8. According to its own charter, Hamas describes itself as a "humanistic movement" which "takes care of human rights and is guided by Islamic tolerance when dealing with the followers of other religions" *as long as followers of other religions do not challenge the supremacy of Islam.* Readers should consider how this sharply contrasts with the interpretation, legal practice, and civil rights of religious freedom in most Western societies, both those with Judeo-Christian foundational law and other modern secular societies. Between 2018-2020, several Gazan-based grassroots youth-led peace and intercultural dialogue movements—aimed to peacefully connect with Israel and other nations' cultural ambassadors—was violently oppressed by Hamas authorities (ie. beatings, financial punishment, imprisonment, deportation).

Christmas Armistice

"And may the peace of Christ reign in your hearts, because it is for this that you were called together in one body. Always be thankful." (Colossians 3:15 – NJB)

America,
Again on the home front, we find ourselves warring.
Today of all days can there be peace?

We all know the fighting will go on
We have all dug into our respective trenches.

There is still plenty,
Ammunition and provisions:
We can choose which to bring to the no-man's-land between our hearts.

Can we build a makeshift bridge
Good enough,
One day or night at a time,
An amicable armistice,

Invite our neighbors to the table
Neighbors long ignored,
Some forgotten as foreigners
Though they are our ancestral brethren?

1. The Christmas Truce of WWI (Great War) was an informal armistice that spontaneously occurred, some arranged, during Christmas Eve and Christmas Day, 1914, all along no-man's land and a great show of common humanity. This included German, French, and British soldiers leaving their respective trenches to swap rations, exchange holiday cheer and well wishes, show pictures of wives and girlfriends and family, and caroling. Joint burials of the dead trapped in no-man's land occurred, along with prisoner swaps and games of soccer (football). A few similar events were reported on the Eastern Front between Russians and Austro-Hungarian armies, though not as extensive. Military commanders and government officials on both sides forbid future events so the war could continue.

The Politics of Christmas

Peace for others is not gained by removing the opportunity for peace in your own heart.

They gathered dishes, languages, prayer, traditions and songs from across the old Commonwealth, the American Prairie, and the Holy Land, but there are no politics here. The conversation freely flowing from the various dishes' symbolism—like Polish *Wigilia* first-star spotting—to the year's accomplishments, pleasure pursuits, news of children, business and professional success, and life's small, often crucial, milestones. A genial mutual appreciation is passed around the great room, because, how absurd it would be to outcompete another in joy.

Hearty dishes and delicacies from Poland, India, Britain, Canada, Caribbean and Mediterranean, all sheltered under and Polish roof, sitting around a Royal Stewart Tartan[1] clad table. This year's wreath resembling a golden laurel crown, like those of the ancient poets. The traditional Advent purples, pinks, reds and greens substituted for candles of various hues of white, cream and pale yellow, as everyone present declares to the table, and in private prayers, intentions to renew their spirit. Each pillar's flames dance, echoing the Yuletide Revels[2] and even Diwali's[3] elation. Though freshly stemmed into the wreath this night, synchronistically, the four candles burn at different speeds, as though each candle had been lite individually over the Advent month.

We each carry unique radiance of the Light. Yet as Szymborska said, "We are children of our age, it's political age...whether you like it or not," and "apolitical poems are also political." [4]. So, earlier this evening many of us assembled inevitably *learned* from the news, that Christmas is not about the light in the dark, or sharing warm radiance despite depression's cold cloak. Christmas light is now political. Everyone must join in darkness, and suffer, because some suffer, a privation typically reserved for Easter. But we also meditated on this.

Abstaining from Christmas, obstructing Christmas spirit, will not take down border walls, refugee camp barbed wire, or resurrect the dead. A weak pacifism is simply moral cowardice, incognito.

1. Royal Stewart, the "everyman's tartan", and personal tartan of the longest serving (1952-2022) British monarch, Queen Elizabeth II. Also unofficially adopted as the "Christmas tartan" or "holiday plaid" in many current/former British Commonwealth countries and in the United States. The Scottish Tartan was originally commissioned by "Bonnie" Prince Charlie (Charles Edward Stewart), an 18th Century heir to the usurped Catholic Throne of Britain (England, Scotland, Ireland), a result of the English civil wars and Scottish wars of independence. Prince Charlie was great-grandson of King John (Jan) III Sobieski of Poland, liberator of Vienna (1683) from the Ottoman siege. Commander of the Jacobite Rising in 1745, and the disastrous Battle of Culloden. The collapse of Jacobite movement directly led to Prince Charlie becoming a degenerate and possibly violent alcoholic, ruining his marriage, and becoming estranged from his children, and died on the same day as his father. Many of the Culloden survivors (Scots, English, Irish) who were not executed, were sentenced for "treason" and punished with "transportation" (exile to the colonies, and removal of citizenship). Others were driven out by anti-Catholic persecution and removal of their civil rights. These events had a direct impact on language, rights and principles formed in the American Constitution and Declaration of Independence. Nearly 1/3 Culloden survivors were sent to Colonial America, mainly North Carolina. Many of them volunteered to fight as minutemen against the British in the American Revolution. The majority of those with Scottish heritage in the United States descend from these Catholic (Highlander) and Presbyterian (Scottish Lowlanders), and Anglicans (Northern English) collaborators. It's estimated that 20-25 million Americans have Scottish descent, and 27-30 million are Scots-Irish (a related ethnic group from Ulster, Ireland).

2. Traditional feasting, carnival, and winter holiday celebration of British/Celtic nations and peoples in the United Kingdom. Often comprising of dancing, theater, comedy, formal performance, feasting.

3. Hindu festival of light which typically corresponds with the Winter Solstice, Hanukkah and Christmas seasons in the West and Latin liturgical calendar.

4. *Children of the Age*, Wislawa Szymborska (Polish Nobel Laureate).

Wigilia
(Polish Christmas Eve, 2019)

In the Dark Night
The first star guides those pilgrimaging to the messenger.

Empty plate, Ancestors remembered,
Empty chair, for the unexpected guest.

Oplatki, breaking the old bread, humble, unleavened,
Blessings around the room.

Twelve dishes, twelve months,
A promise to feed ourselves and each other round the year.

Krupnik to warm the soul.
From the dark Earth, humus and rot,

Spirits dance with fire herbs.
We raise a glass to Mary, in the spirit of *Mokosh* and our mothers.

When the veil between the animal and human world is thin,
On to *Pasterka*, Midnight Mass,

To contemplate
Our instinctual mortal and Divine nature, and remember

The unexpected guest, intercessor of Fate.

1. *Wigilia* (Polish pronunciation: [vʲiˈgʲilja]) refers to the Polish Christian
    Christmas Eve and its festivities, especially the traditional dishes,
    Christmas Eve Midnight Mass (*Pasterka*), tree decorating, communal
    blessings *Oplatki*, and gift giving. *Krupnik*, often called "fire vodka",
    specially prepared by the host for Polish Christmas Eve toasts, is honey
    vodka blended with mulling spices. *Mokosh* is the pre-Christian Slavic
    spirit of hearth, home and hospitality, is still seen in the notable Polish
    hospitality customs.

Christmas Renewal
(December 2021)

"But the angel said, 'Do not be afraid. Look, I bring you news of great joy, a joy to be shared by the whole people.'" (Luke 2:10 - NJB)

The town criers of the left and right have us believing a new piece of
        community fractures off each day,
And the middle ground implodes.

     Long lay the world, in sin and error pining...

I am in my kitchen preparing all 12 traditional Polish *Wigilia* dishes.
Two years of plague and quarantines, with a brief reprieve for
Christmas.

     The weary world rejoices...

The ICU nurses and doctors' heroic efforts, despite exhaustion.
The masses screaming for 11th hour magic elixirs.
A Filipino family prays in the ER lobby for their ailing child.

     Fall on your knees, oh hear the angels' voices...

Paranoia gossip spreads around town.
Vehemence toward kin of different persuasion.
The chant of conspiracy slogans fills the airwaves.

     Sweet hymns of joy in grateful chorus raise we...

In these moments we understand
How much we need Christmas.

Snowbound
(December 26th, South Shore of Lake Superior)

"Sophia, or the archetypal feminine of the *imago Dei,* provides a sense of love and connection to a caring, responsive matrix within the world that bridges the intellect to the emotional heart. This is needed for a true relationship with the divine, the self."[1]

Fifteen friends gather in a snowbound lodge for some late Yule revelry. Hanging on the hearth, among an assemblage of cross-stitch, applique and decoupage designs, is my stocking. The knitting resembles Fair Isle patterns, but embarrassingly, was likely woven by people who haven't seen a kilt since Queen Victoria's regiments marched through their jungles. What can I do now but honor their skill and labor by using it as gift bearer, traditions tool, and history teacher?

The solstice's darkness still rings us, and the polar vortex plunges the mercury to -20F. Then the unceasing ice wind chills the air to -40F, but it does not freeze our spirits or the jokes.

I have prepared a mélange of parody Christmas and Solstice carols, poetry and improv comedy skits (mostly roasting myself and my friends). Others have brought a potlach of gifts and food to share, helping us all slow down. Clove-spiced tea, a coffee French Press, Italian Roast Espresso, real cacao and a local farmer's fresh milk. Guitars, saxophones, hand drums, opera-trained voices. Cranberry and orange scones, fresh fruit, traditional and global treats. Novels, poetry, sketch books, paints and small canvases. Seasonal music from Scotland, Ireland, Wales, Bavaria and old Hebrew celebration songs. Baking and cooking experimental essentials.

Despite the sizable A-frame white pine log lodge's cathedral ceilings and wall of windows, fulling spanning the shore-side wall, and ample space to find cozy corners, sprawling couches and typical nap-sized La-Z-Boy's, cabin fever inevitably settles into our bones. By the second day everyone becomes a bit fruitcake. Our resident chef decides to brave the polar vortex and fire up the Webber kettle (just to get outside), but struggles to keep the charcoals hot enough to properly sear the steaks and chicken short of two hours.

The men, wanting fresh air, layer up with every piece of winter gear they brought (now discovered inadequate) and struggle to trek the ice-wave-sculpted shore for a mile before some decide cigars in the closed garage is a more sensible plan. The next two days are spent in, mostly, stunning silence of the fast rolling clouds making the sun dance across the shoreline's thick snow crust. I'm held in awe, as the rarely frozen Lake Superior has turned into an Arctic-like ice shelf, stretching beyond the low-slung sun horizon.

1. Jankowski, Vanessa (2024). *Modern Challenges of Consciousness According to Jung, Hillman, von Franz, and Woodman.* p. 137 (Publication No. 31560901) [Doctoral dissertation, Pacifica Graduate Institute]. ProQuest Dissertations Publishing. https://www.proquest.com/pqdtglobal1/dissertations-theses/modern-challenges-consciousness-according-jung/docview/3101097202/sem-2?accountid=45402 .

New Year's Up North
(an ode to Northern Michigan, the 1980s-1990s)

After the winter factory lay-off, or generous union vacation, our Polish, German, Cherokee and Scots-Irish family clan is making the post-Christmas trek Up North from Flint, Detroit and Indianapolis, for skiing, ice fishing, snowmobiling, sledding, or in some years, daredevil open-water ice skiing. New Year's Eve, up the icy stone stairs to the hilltop cottage, windows still alit with Christmas twinkle lights. Last year, the normally inky charcoal sky parted with the Northern Lights dancing Irish-green ribbons.

A celebration is gathering—neighbors, friends, family, from up and down the lake-side street. From a deck high above the road, Uncle Joel lights classic Chinese fireworks, smuggled from Indiana. Then hustling back to the kitchen, he collects and triumphantly lays out platter after platter of artistically presented and delectable *hors d'oeuvre*. The joys of hosting are engraved in the wrinkles on the old man's face.

Piled together on Uncle Joel's convertible bench-bed, my cousins and I silently watch from the three-season porch's 270-degree windows overlooking the lake. The small space heater keeps us eight to ten youngsters from being completely blue-nosed and complaining. The 12-inch color TV—brought out on a microwave cart with a VCR, and movies rented from the convenience-video-liquor-bait-bakery-grocery store—entertains us well till midnight. We're still adolescent enough to marvel at the colored universe outside: swirling sparks, the soft glowing heavens, and the joyful New Year's sprit that embraces all. Still too naïve to understand the adults' jokes (not to mention we were sequestered, to be unheard but still seen) we had selected our own films for the TV—*Earnest Saves Christmas* and *Wayne's World* and *Encino Man*, in order to create our own circle of mirth.

Meanwhile, between fresh shuffles of Polish-style Rummy, Spoons, Euchre and unique poker games invented by Grandpa Joe and Great-Uncle Frank (both long gone to the grave), the adults exchange round-after-round of stored up Midnight Mass inappropriate stories and jabs and jokes. Several around the felt table take the betting a bit too seriously (the Svedka, Coors, Busch not helping) trying to toss their year-end tradesmen's bonuses into the pot, much to the exasperation of their wives and girlfriends.

Even my eighty-year-old grandmother and her sisters enjoy more than a few highballs or glasses of Crown, their soft felt purple and gold bags now holding most of the table's winnings. All the while, these card-shark crones are listening with cocked heads and squinting eyes to the others' specious proclamations and inflated resolutions. All jokes stopped at ten minutes to twelve and as everyone directed their full attention and breathless respect to Dick Clark.

America's midnight M.C. was already well past retirement age, but still enthusiastic and vibrant about New York's eminent countdown, the only clock to best England's Greenwich for the world's most relevant timekeeper—indeed, God's own annual hourglass turner. The same silly Victorian-esque paper hats and tiaras were passed out just before streamers were tossed, party poppers cracked, whistles caused grandma to pull out her hearing aid, and Robbie Burns's *Auld Lang Syne* was sung and mumbled throughout the cabin. "Should old acquaintance be forgot and never brought to mind?"...For *auld lang syne* my long-departed dears.

Auld Lang Syne
(for my pipe teacher, and her teacher, and their teacher...)

Should old acquaintance be forgot, and never brought to mind?

Blessings almost appear to belong to a dying art of welcoming
Spirit into sanctify the spaces between us.

Elders blessings withheld.
Brotherly benedictions,
Sisterly salutations,
Unsaid.

And surely you'll buy your pint cup, and surely I'll buy mine?

We are a generation deprived,
Amazing grace not expressed at table.
Growing up, but not raised,
In homes without blessings.

But we've wandered many a weary foot, since days of auld lang syne...

We are a generation depriving ourselves, and those who follow.
For blessings elevate the soul beyond the spirit of the times.
And so our homes remain unhallowed ground.

For so many youth, the road ahead is often nihilism's icy crags,
The burning frost senselessly ruptured bonds.
Guideless, rootless, their dreams become delusions, like a landmark
        of drifting snow.
But this new year, why fill our tables with frosty demeanors?

We two have paddled in the stream from morning sun till dine, but seas between us
        broad have roared since auld lang syne.

Before the year turns, I'll accept my first pipes,
Reach across the lands to take a trusted hand
In the great circle with my teacher, and all the pipers before her,
All our hands crossing our hearts as we reel and remember *auld lang*
        syne,

Turning to face each other, and the world again.

So I'll take that cup of kindness yet, for *auld lang syne!*

Winter In-Perpetua

Those old souls
Staring at the cold isolation of the post-modern world
Over populated with nothing, and everything, at the same time.

Cold-Burning
(January 2022)

A pair of exuberant greyhounds are loosed on a clear royal-blue
winter day.

I marvel as the dogs almost float across the fresh fallen powder,
Coursing after a brash squirrel who has dared to enter their
kingdom.

As they gave chase around our yard,
Faster than a Canadian Bombardier Rotax at full throttle,
Their paws plume the snow, like a snowmobile mountain paddle
track.

These streamlined speed creatures, like living art deco sculptures,
Bob and weave between the dormant Crimson King Maple, Catalpa,
and White Spire Birch
    (like stanchions at a Ski-Doo snowcross course).
There are no Arctic Cats here, just the neighbors' bold grey tabby,
And the occasional bobcat that ranges down from Minnesota,
    (not to mention a very-lost mountain lion that made the bird
feeder into a toy one
    summer).

That night, the first new moon of the year,

I walked out into the near-zero chill,
So cold, even the heaven's-reaching oaks and black locus don't creek,
    (even they must be still to conserve their own heat).

Rosary in hand, I pray,
Mother of God,
Melt the ice in all our hearts
For having betrayed each other
In these time of cold-burning.

Glow
(Solemnity of Mary, January 1)

The midnight glowing, sheen
Slick, ice-crusted snow
Coats our neighborhood
Like the Creator's special seasonal fondant.

The world was not intended to be half-baked,
So the cosmic confectioner
Prepared a royal baby shower.
We're all awaiting the wise guest's arrival
But love is the center of attention.

The Mother is doing what all mothers do,
Meditating, in moments of post-partum bliss,
Already glimpsing the future,
The veil is still thin; being connected, yet outside oneself.

Preparing for the Solemnity of Mary
We wait
Inside the sweetness.

We wait,
Mid-winter stillness,
Silence.

The Aftermath of Christmas

"Truth came to the market but did not sell because people wanted to buy lies." -
African Proverb

The aftermath of Christmas is not Christmas.
Instead, the carnage of a savage cash register).

Not a time of rest.
Katabasis, hitting bottom.[1]

A brief moment of consciousness,
Leaving many wondering, *Was it worth it?*
Until the next holiday,
Like Clockwork, you will submit.[2]
No sense in continuing this cute consumer hunger strike.

How about that New Year's Resolution?
Yes, yes, a cleanse sounds good!
Perhaps a cerebral colonoscopy,
To detox from New Year's Day football commercials?

I am walking through aisle after aisle,
Just a portion of warehouse after warehouse,
Supplied by cargo ship after cargo ship,
Filled by factory city after factory city,
Energized by despondent human machine after human machine.
All wondering, year after year, *Where does it all go?*[3]

Poseidon's palace.
On a container ship piloted by Prometheus,
Hephaestus's latest creations will eventually put him (and everyone
else) out of work.
With such tools
The destiny of mortals is beyond
Apollonian calculation, Athenian imagination or convenient
Artemesian "arrangement".[4]

Then again,
Perhaps it isn't so foolish to take weather advice from a groundhog.
Even the least among us, with their hearts closest to the earth, *know*.

1. *Katabasis* (Ancient Greek: "descent to the underworld"). Need to further define according to geology, meteorology, and C.G. Jung.
2. *A Clockwork Orange*, a film by Stanley Kubrick, depicts the torture/treatment of a violent and sadistic psychopath/sociopath by means of sensory overload, psychopharmacology, and Classical Pavlovian/Behavior Therapy.
3. "For the sellers, understanding the custom, put forth all kinds of trumpery, and whatever, being useless and ridiculous, they have been unable to sell throughout the year they now sell as an Exmas gift..." C.S. Lewis, *Xmas and Christmas: A Lost chapter from Herodotus.*
4. Through a Depth Psychology lens, the Greek Goddess Artemis is the perpetual virgin, aka. juvenile feminine development. Among her "shadow" (immature) personality aspects are the *inability* to engage in intimate relationships, lack of emotional vulnerability and when offended, she often punishes and attacks without mercy.

Groundhog Day

"You never know how much you really believe anything until its truth or falsehood becomes a matter of life and death to you." - C.S. Lewis

Each year on Groundhog Day, I challenge a group of my clients to get off the wheel of suffering. Whether they're trapped on the addiction wheel, the loneliness ladder (going nowhere up and down), riding the downward spiral of Samsara, lost in an existential labyrinth, or experiencing some other "rinse-repeat" relapse cycle, I task them to bushwhack through their B.S. I provoke them to leave the habits of scrolling past their life, avoiding commitment, by way of quickly flicking their attention to the right or left, and occasionally snapping back to the dreary one-way sidewalks where everyone else in their social circle seems to be (rarely examining the fertile middle roads).

Yet they persist, fixating on chasing unicorn solutions, mistaking magical thinking for inspired practical change. Instead, tracing over their circle of "ego death" with remaining bits of well-worn chalk (a street corner outline of their future). Or, spasmodically gyrating up and down the ever-spinning ego barber pole, while also chasing "true blue" and "real red" stripes—paths that never intersect unless they pour into the ocean of tradition.[2] I nearly beg them to cease their latest "30-day challenge" (virtually same as the last) toward repetitive regression. I remind them how they mistake trends, crazes and everyone's-doing-it fix-all-philosophies as legitimate exit ramps from their personal highway to hell.

I tell them about Bill Murray's character in this holiday's vintage classic film, *Groundhog Day*. Murray portrays a cynical man who could not connect with or inspire anyone. A "self-made" man primarily concerned with making himself *just as he likes*. A man who would have quoted J.P. Sartre as guru, and Sartre's famous line, "hell is other people," as his personal motto. A few of the women and girls openly note this is all *just as much a women's problem*, no matter how much they want to think Sophia is their *personal* and *exclusive* patron saint or goddess, and they are immune from arrogance and self-delusion ego trips because they lack a Y-chromosome, or have changed their gender identity, or relabeled their pronouns.

Curmudgeon Bill's transformation in *Groundhog Day* was exiting from his self-made hell. His well-scripted and stereotyped career did not save him, nor his quippy-talking-point-sarcasm. Begrudgingly showing up for the community rituals only fed his guarded isolation.

110

Even suicide proved no solution to the problems an ego-dominated personality and entertainment-lust create. I challenge them to stop being "self-made" wo(men), and instead discerning vocation, start building community, and *let life make them* as they challenge themselves to answer their True calling.

1. Groundhog Day (aka. Candlemas) is the traditional end of the Christmas Season in the United States and functions as another folklore/pagan fortune telling day. Candlemas celebrates the presentation of the Jesus Christ child at the Temple (Luke 2:23-24) to the elders and the messianic predictions by the prophet Simeon (who some scholars say was also blind). The rituals of reading the groundhog's (aka. "Punxsutawney Phil") actions, or willingness to "see his shadow" and be frightened or not, back into his hole, is part of the annual ritual of reading the signs in the natural world. The tradition was started by Pennsylvania Dutch and Germans who brought their European Badger-based seasonal weather forecasting as a form of reading signs in nature. The actual "interpretation" of the groundhog's action sign is said to closely follow the annual predictions in the American publication *Farmer's Almanac.*

2. "A tide of stories, deep and wide, where echoes of the past reside, I dive into the ocean's heart, to feel the rhythm, play my part." *Into the Ocean of Tradition,* poem by Jericho Brown, Pulitzer Prize Winner.

A Pagan, a Christian and a Post-Christian Modern Walk into a Recording Studio with Kabir and C.S. Lewis

"People [who] have their inner eyes of conscience blind; they don't see who is real and who [and what] is fake." – Kabir[1]

Those over-sung carols, they will not bring you joy.
But there are meta-verses whose
Meaning has presently escaped you.[2, 3, 4]
Slow your holiday (and daily) rush.
They are in plain sight.

You must listen more deeply[3, 4]
for long-unsung carols and chants,
Some forgotten,
Some your grandparents barely recalled when they were young.
Others perhaps sung in a tongue your grandparents-grandparents
        forgot
Before they left primary school.

That sardonic and cynical humor will not relieve you of your sad
        condition.[5]
We satire the traditions because we have forgotten how to be
        together.
But mockery is a poor lock pick
To break the tension
Restraining your hearts' tongue.

Dear ones, stop
Pretending tolerance, which is ignorance of love.
Throughout the year, cease
Dedicating your studies to learning what Kabir calls "terrific
        talking".[3, 6]
Both of these shut iron gates to the heart.[7]
One cannot grasp the meaning of Christmas with a mind that
        remains grey and loveless,[5, 6]
A heart empty of song.

I say to the artists,
Want to make a song for the ages, not just this age? [6, 8, 9, 10]
We don't need any more ice-slick lyrics, or
Rebranding doldrum rhythms into glitter snowflake sensations.
The culture of cool is already global and ever-present.
Remixing sexual sleet to fly across the stage, in every way
        imaginable,

Will not birth a new hope for ourselves, humanity, or a creative
      renaissance.[8, 9, 10]
Stylizing cheap-taboo titillation can only form ice queen icons.
These are not the joy of Christmas.[2, 3, 9]

Dear ones,
You must stop knowing nothing, or acting simultaneously ignorant
      and innocent,
About Christmas.[2, 10]

1.   Kabir was born during a time of extreme social and religious polarization in the Indian subcontinent. Much of his work and poetry was dedicated to bringing people of different paths together (especially Muslims and Hindus)—(ie.) "The Hindu says Ram is beloved, the Muslim says Rahim. They fight and kill each other, no one gets the point."
2.   In C.S. Lewis's "Chronicles of Narnia: the Lion, the Witch and the Wardrobe" (p.118), the character of Father Christmas provides the children with "tools not toys," things with long-effective importance and utility for the challenges they will face on their journey. Father Christmas (i.e. Santa Clause in other cultures) or the wise elder gift giver, did not provide *mere entertainment*.
3.   "Hence a Pagan, though in many ways merrier than a modern, had a deep sadness. When he asked himself what was wrong with the world he did not immediately reply, 'the social system,' or 'our allies,' or 'education.' It occurred to him that he himself might be one of the things that was wrong with the world." C.S. Lewis (1946), *A Christmas Sermon for Pagans*. Strand Magazine, vol. 112, Issue 672.
4.   "And this leads us to the third great difference between a Pagan and a post-Christian man. Believing in a real Right and Wrong means finding out that you are not very good." C.S. Lewis (1946), *A Christmas Sermon for Pagans*. Strand Magazine, vol. 112, Issue 672.
5.   S.A.D. – Seasonal Affective Disorder. In the Northern Hemisphere, this manifests as a typically depressive condition correlated to the Winter Season (Diagnostics and Statistics Manual of Psychology, DSM). The onset of the condition is related to a combination of psycho-social developmental factors (i.e. "maturity"), historically negative associations with the Winter season, drop in natural Vitamin D from the significantly less sunlight exposure, monotone/greyscale landscape (sensory deprivation), significant reduction in physical activity and higher-energy producing metabolic and adrenal cycles, poor quality diet/nutrition, and real or imagined feelings of social isolation
6.   *The Spiritual Athlete*, Kabir. (ed.) R. Bly, J. Hillman, M. Meade. (1992) "The Rag and Bone Shop of the Heart". Harper Perennial.
7.   *Knowing Nothing Shuts the Iron Gates*. (ed.) R. Bly, J. Hillman, M. Meade. (1992) "The Rag and Bone Shop of the Heart". Harper Perennial.
8.   "But what Hecataeus says, that Exmas and Crissmas are the same, it is not credible... [I]t is not likely that men, even being barbarians, should suffer so many and great things in honour of a god they do not believe in..." [1] C.S. Lewis, "Xmas and Christmas: A Lost Chapter from

Herodotus," *God in the Dock* (Grand Rapids, MI: William B. Eerdmans Publishing Co., 1970), pp. 301-303. Lewis originally published his essay in 1954, well before what many current writers would consider to be an era of "modern problems", nihilism, post-modern psycho-spiritual malaise, multiple "lost generations".

9. "Now the *post-Christian* [my emphasis added] view...is quite different. According to it Nature is not a live thing to be reverenced: it is a kind of machine for us to exploit. There is no objective Right or Wrong: each race or class can invent its own code or 'ideology' just as it pleases. And whatever may be amiss with the world, it is certainly not we, not the ordinary people; it is up to God (if, after all, He should happen to exist), or to Government or to Education, to give us what we want. They are the shop, we are the customers: and 'the customer is always right.'" C.S. Lewis (1946), *A Christmas Sermon for Pagans*. Strand Magazine, vol. 112, Issue 672.

10. "If there is no objective standard, then our choice between one ideology and another becomes a matter of arbitrary taste. Our battle for democratic ideals against Nazi [fascist] ideals has been a waste of time, because the one is no better than the other." C.S. Lewis (1946), *A Christmas Sermon for Pagans*. Strand Magazine, vol. 112, Issue 672.

Author's Bio

Kyle grew up in Flint, Michigan in the 1980s-2000s as the American Auto Industry, economy, schools, social services and local community began to collapse. Born to a large extended Polish/ Scottish-American family of auto workers, military veterans, construction workers, nurses and other skilled trades, Kyle witnessed the first-hand suffering of the American Rustbelt de-industrialization, off-shoring of jobs, betrayal of labor, urban blight and inevitable class and racial violence. He credits his many teachers, mentors and adoptive families for helping him *not* succumb to the fatalism, despair and decay around him.

Despite his extensive training as a clinician and in academia—University of Chicago (AM/MSW), Pacifica Graduate Institute (MA Jungian/Depth Psychology), University of Michigan (BSW), and a 5-year post-graduate advanced clinical training program—it is his Polish and Scottish heritage, his marriage to Vanessa (a brilliant clinician, artist and PhD. scholar in her own right), studies in world religions/philosophy, his Catholic (Universal Church) faith, being an avid lifelong history buff, traveling and the many ordinarily interesting people that have crossed his path (in clinic and community) that most informs his poetry and other writing. Kyle's clinical work greatly informs his poetry and his desire to keep it relatable and relevant to a wide population.

Outside the two clinics and training centers, they co-own and operate, and practice full-time psychotherapy, Kyle and Vanessa care for their border-lands property outside Chicago, cultivating and foraging local plants and restoring their small forest plot, and hosting friends, family and speakers/ trainers at their home. Both have several upcoming psychology and poetry books in development. Kyle studies Scottish Highland Bagpipes and saxophone, and Vanessa Native American Flute and violin.

Reader's Notes

www.ingramcontent.com/pod-product-compliance
Lightning Source LLC
Chambersburg PA
CBHW072355090426
42741CB00012B/3042